WE MUST ALL BE READY TO SACRIFICE

The Great War and its Effect
on the People of Freeborn, Mower,
and Steele Counties in Minnesota

DEAN ULLAND

Published in the United States by Fox Pointe Publishing, LLP.

www.foxpointepublishing.com/author-dean-ulland

Library of Congress Cataloging-in-Publication Data
Ulland, Dean, author.
Olson, Sarah, editor.
Hudson, Becca, designer.

We Must All Be Ready to Sacrifice:
The Great War and its Effect on the People of Freeborn,
Mower, and Steele Counties in Minnesota
Dean Ulland. - First edition

Summary: A history of southern Minnesota during World War I.
ISBN (hardcover) 978-1-952567-12-4 / (softcover) 978-1-952567-13-1
[1. History - United States Midwest. 2. History - World War I.
3. History - United States.]
Library of Congress Control Number: 2 0 2 1 9 0 8 0 0 0

Printed and bound in the United States of America by Lakeside Press Inc.
First printing May 2021

For Our Grandchildren:

Liam, Carter, Winifred, Jackson, Esme,
Penelope, Graham, and Bennett

CONTENTS

PROLOGUE

WORLD WAR I, 1914-1918, is undoubtedly one of the most important events of the modern era. Ten million soldiers and five million civilians died. Twenty million were wounded, many of them suffering long-term ill effects from their time on the battlefield. The monetary cost was staggering. Still today, humanity endures the effects of industrialized warfare. Together with the Protestant Reformation and the French Revolution, historians consider World War I, in its short four years, as one of the most important geopolitical and world historical events of the last millennium.

Countless volumes have been written about the geopolitical, militaristic, and economic causes and effects of the war. Scholars often focused their research on leaders and the way they responded to big events. In other words, history from the top down. All of that is important. There is much to be learned about the turn of events that caused such a catastrophe. However, I believe people, not events, make history. The story of these events, as important as they are on a world historical scale, often do not provide enough details about people caught up in the war. What about the young men who left their farms and families, jobs and sweethearts, to serve and sometimes die in a foreign war? What was life like for those young men as they were drafted, trained, and sent across seas to distant battlefields? What of the people who stayed home? How did they respond to the news of the war? Was everyone united in the war effort? How did the work get done with so many young men gone? What about local and state politics? How did schools and churches function? This book will consider those questions and more. The idea is to connect the big events of the war to the lives of ordinary Minnesotans. In other words, history on a community and individual level.

The book will focus on the people and events in part of southern Minnesota. Specifically, it will discuss the people living within about a 30 mile radius of Blooming Prairie in southeastern Steele County, the geographic hub of the four-county area which includes Freeborn, Mower, Steele, and Dodge Counties, and the cities of Albert Lea, Austin, and Owatonna, as well as the smaller communities and farms nearby. While most of the events in this book occurred in southern Minnesota, the lessons learned can be applied more broadly to greater Minnesota, the Midwest, and the entire United States.

Everyone had to adapt to wartime conditions, and the process was sometimes painful. Both the state and federal government sought to unite citizens in the great patriotic crusade. Yet not everyone believed in the cause. Sometimes German-Americans were reluctant to fully support the war, arguing instead for a policy of U.S. neutrality. Minnesota members of the Nonpartisan League and its leaders, including Charles Lindbergh, were opposed to the war, and occasionally were treated harshly for their opposition. Various businesses, including some in the liquor trade, were forced to shut down.

For Minnesotans, and all Americans, the process of going to war, then fighting and winning it, was tumultuous. Yet, resilient people came together to work for what they believed to be a just cause. This is their story.

1

EUROPE 1914-1917

"A friend came to see me on one of the evenings of the last week — he thinks it was on Monday, August 3rd. We were standing at a window of my room in the Foreign Office. It was getting dusk, and the lamps were being lit in the space below on which we were looking. My friend recalls that I remarked on this with the words: "The lamps are going out all over Europe, we shall not see them lit again in our life-time."

–Sir Edward Grey, British Foreign Minister[1]

"What is this war other than a war of extermination? The loser will be the one who first exhausts all his moral and material resources."

–Charles de Gaulle[2]

"Far and near and low and louder
On the roads of earth go by,

1. Grey of Fallodon, *Twenty-Five Years: 1892-1916*. (New York, Frederick A. Stokes Company 1925), *20*.
2. Charles de Gaulle, letter to his mother, December 1914. Julian Jackson, *De Gaulle*. (Cambridge, Massachusetts: Belknap Press of Harvard University Press 2018), 35.

Dear to friends and food for powder,
Soldiers marching all to die."
–*A Shropshire Lad*, A.E. Houseman

"...he was right. And the world was not what it had been.
It was at an end." –Joseph Roth[3]

Grey the diplomat, de Gaulle the soldier, Houseman the scholar, and Roth the novelist were correct. The summer of 1914 brought an abrupt end to centuries of tradition. Political ideas and technological developments spawned in the nineteenth century brought radical changes to the twentieth. Nothing would ever be the same for Europe or for the world.

Soldiers marched away to war, and millions of them died. By 1919, the glittering courts of the Habsburg, Romanov, and Hohenzollern dynasties had all collapsed. In truth, many were not sad to see them go. They were antiques, relics of a bygone era, unsuited to the twentieth century. After the war, they were tragically replaced by authoritarians, fanatics, and extremists. Men like Lenin, Stalin, and Hitler climbed to power, willing to use any means necessary to impose their vision of the future on the demoralized and impoverished peoples of central and eastern Europe.

In France, the charm and optimism of the Belle Époque, or "Beautiful Era," did not just fade away—it was eradicated virtually overnight, replaced by previously unimaginable ugliness and horror. The war cost 1.7 million French citizens their lives, and much of Northeastern France was in ruins.

The "Irish Question" and women's suffrage in Britain dominated headlines, highlighting the difficult discourse capturing the public's attention. The new Labour Party was flexing its muscles.

3. Joseph Roth, *The Radetzky March*. (London, Granta Books 2003), 207.

Workers, long shut out of the political system, were demanding and receiving a voice. In Britain too, the ancient signposts which had marked the way for centuries, were lost. It seemed that change was in the air everywhere. However, few people sensed that one of the greatest and most terrible agents of change was near.

In the spring of 1914, Europeans had good reason to look to the future with confidence. After a long period of sluggishness, many European countries experienced economic growth, and industrial production was expanding. People had money to spend, and trade barriers were generally relaxed. New categories of industrial and consumer goods were readily available at affordable prices. Extensive rail networks and fast, modern ships quickly and affordably moved raw materials, finished goods, and people. Communication by telegraph and telephone was common, and cables crisscrossed the oceans of the world. Whispers of the wireless radio enchanted inventors everywhere. Bankers in London and New York controlled unprecedented amounts of capital which financed projects across the globe. Railroads, dams, factories, and more were being built, sometimes in unlikely places. It seemed that anything was possible. In fact, the world was so interconnected and interdependent economically that some, like British author Norman Angell, thought war was impossible.[4]

Angell was wrong. Despite the growing worldwide prosperity and cooperation, war came, first to Europe, then to the Mideast, Africa, and the oceans of the world. Eventually, most of the world was affected.

Factories that could have been used for productive, peaceful purposes instead built weapons. The Krupp works in Germany,

4. Norman Angell, *The Great Illusion: A Study of the Relation of Military Power to National Advantage.* (New York, London: G.P. Putnam's sons 1910), 44-45.

Skoda in Austria-Hungary, Vickers in Great Britain, and many other manufacturers used their engineering prowess to produce large numbers of accurate weapons with high rates of fire that were capable of inflicting enormous numbers of casualties.

What happened? What caused this horror? Why did prosperous European nations squander the blood of millions and incur huge debts, some of which are still being paid a century later?

Why, in 1917, was it in the American national interest to join the conflict? Young men in the prime of their lives, from farms and hamlets like Corning/Red Oak Grove, Taopi, Moscow, and Bixby, went to war. Thousands from small towns like Twin Lakes, Blooming Prairie, Adams and larger cities including Albert Lea, Austin and Owatonna, found their names on draft rosters. All were sent to fight on European battlefields 4,000 miles from home, some to be scarred for life, and some never to return.

Many factors played a role in the outbreak of war. Nationalism, militarism, and the alliance system (which existed in Europe in 1914) all contributed to the hostilities. The specific trigger, however, was a murder in Sarajevo, the capital of Bosnia.

Bosnia, on the Balkan Peninsula in southeastern Europe, was a province of the Austro-Hungarian Empire in 1914. For centuries, Bosnia had been part of the Ottoman Empire.

In the age of imperialism, powerful nations sought to expand their spheres of influence at the expense of weaker nations and peoples. The Ottoman Turks controlled vast swaths of territory in the Middle East, and a part of the Balkan peninsula (including Bosnia) in southeastern Europe. However, at the dawn of the 20th century, their grip was weakening. After a long period of decline, the Ottoman Empire, widely considered the "Sick man of Europe," was weak and unable to defend its empire.

In 1908, under a strange set of circumstances, Austria-Hungary made a deal with Russia and formally annexed Bosnia. The 1908 seizure destroyed the fiction of Ottoman sovereignty. The Ottomans were not consulted, and the wishes of the Bosnian people were not considered. Years of diplomatic initiatives aimed at pacifying the volatile region were upset.

Ethnically and religiously, many Bosnians were aligned with their independent, eastern neighbors in Serbia. With nationalistic aspirations of their own for the Balkan Peninsula, the Serbs wanted Bosnia to be a part of Greater Serbia. To compound the problem, there had long been animosity between the Serbs and Austria-Hungary. They differed culturally, ethnically, and linguistically. Diplomatically, Serbia was aligned with Russia; Austria-Hungary was an ally of Germany. Austro-Hungarians were predominantly Catholic; Serbs were Orthodox and Muslim. Economically, a trade dispute over Serbian pork, labelled the "Pig War" of 1906, almost caused a shooting war between Russia and Austria-Hungary. To put it mildly, they did not get along. Those differences made Austria-Hungary's Balkan acquisition a particularly contentious move in the eyes of Serbia's leaders.

Radical Serbian nationalists were determined that the Bosnian annexation would not stand. A shadowy organization in Serbia with ties to the government known as the "Black Hand," or "Union or Death," surreptitiously armed several young would-be terrorists and smuggled them across the border into Bosnia.

On June 28th, 1914, Archduke Franz Ferdinand, heir to the Austro-Hungarian throne, was visiting Sarajevo with his wife, Sophie. Gavrilo Princip, one of the Serbian terrorists, was seated in a coffeehouse, apparently thinking that he had missed his opportunity to kill the royal couple. He was therefore surprised when the Archduke's chauffeur-driven limousine stopped on the street directly outside the coffeehouse. The driver had taken a wrong turn

The assassination of Franz Ferdinand.
Achille Beltrame, *Domenica del Corriere,*
July 12th, 1914.

and as he was attempting to turn the vehicle around (the automobile was difficult to shift into reverse), Princip rose from his seat, walked out of the coffeehouse, and from a distance of five feet, shot Franz Ferdinand and his wife, killing them both. The shots that rang out reverberated around the world. The echoes are with us still.

Today, it is hard to understand how an assassination in a re-

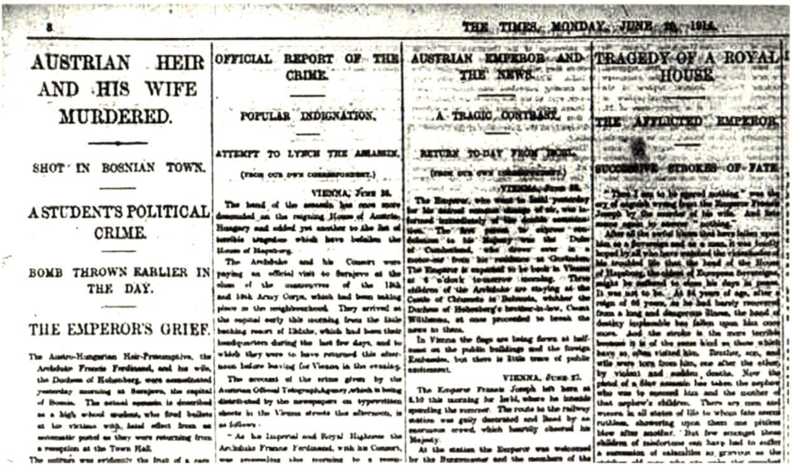

THE TIMES, MONDAY, JUNE 29, 1914.

AUSTRIAN HEIR AND HIS WIFE MURDERED.

SHOT IN BOSNIAN TOWN.

A STUDENT'S POLITICAL CRIME.

BOMB THROWN EARLIER IN THE DAY.

THE EMPEROR'S GRIEF.

OFFICIAL REPORT OF THE CRIME.

POPULAR INDIGNATION.

ATTEMPT TO LYNCH THE ASSASSIN.

(FROM OUR OWN CORRESPONDENT.)

AUSTRIAN EMPEROR AND THE NEWS.

A TRAGIC CONTRAST.

RETURN TO-DAY FROM ISCHL.

(FROM OUR OWN CORRESPONDENT.)

TRAGEDY OF A ROYAL HOUSE.

THE AFFLICTED EMPEROR.

SUCCESSIVE STROKES OF FATE.

The news flashed around the world.
THE TIMES, London, June 29th, 1914.

mote part of Europe could set off a world war. After all, what nation's vital interests were really at stake? It is unlikely that any of the major European powers except for Austria-Hungary really cared about the fate of Bosnia or that of Franz Ferdinand. What was at stake was European geopolitical stability. There were five power centers in Europe in 1914: Great Britain, France, Germany, Austria-Hungary, and Russia. War was unlikely as long as there was a rough perception of equilibrium or balance of power among those five empires. In 1914, those five powers were divided into two great alliances and the longstanding alliance system proved to be fatally flawed.

The first alliance, known as the "Triple Entente," was a friendly association between Great Britain, France, and Russia. The Entente was not a firm military treaty; rather, the signatories agreed they had an obligation to support one another as a general policy. The agreement was vague, but the Entente partners did support each other when war broke out.

The other powers, Germany, Austria-Hungary, and Italy were bound together in the Triple Alliance which was formed by a treaty

EUROPE, 1914 - Lines Drawn.
Map courtesy of the United States Military
Academy Department of History.

signed in 1882. It should be noted that, when war broke out, Italy did not participate as a member of the Triple Alliance, but the Ottomans did. Italy left the Alliance in 1915 and declared war on Austria-Hungary.

There was another alliance in Europe in 1914, or at the very least a close friendship between the Russians and the Serbs. That friendship set the dominoes falling and brought all the great powers of Europe into conflict by August, 1914.

After Franz Ferdinand's assassination, Austria-Hungary was determined to punish Serbia for the murder of their heir and, with the support of allied Germany, issued a humiliating ultimatum to the Serbs on July 23rd, 1914. Austria fully expected Serbia to reject the humiliating demands, at which point they would crush the

Serbs before Russia could intervene. To Austria's surprise, the Serbs agreed to eight of ten of the terms. However, partial acceptance was not enough. Individuals close to the Austrian Emperor pushed for a punitive war with the Serbs. The Emperor Franz Joseph, who had been on the Austro-Hungarian throne since 1848, decided to risk it. After negotiations failed, he signed the declaration of war at his summer palace in Bad Ischl on July 28th, 1914.

The Austrians had reason to be confident of a good outcome in a war with Serbia. Germany had given Austria-Hungary a blank check, that is, a pledge of unconditional support. The Austrians were emboldened knowing Germany could step in should they be losing the upper hand.

For their part, the Serbs had an ally in Russia. The Russian and Serbian people, both of Slavic ethnicity, also had a common religion in Orthodox Christianity. Russia looked on the Serbs as their little Slav brothers and were willing to assist their brothers in a conflict with Austria-Hungary.

By July, European diplomats realized the implications of what had initially seemed to be a local incident. The foreign ministers of the principal European nations, as well as Kaiser Wilhelm of Germany, Czar Nicholas of Russia, and other European officials failed to find any formula for maintaining the peace. No agreement could be reached. The anti-militarist French Socialist, Jean Jaures, tried to organize a general strike of French and German workers in an effort to force their respective governments to negotiate. He failed, and was assassinated in Paris by a French nationalist on the evening of July 31st, 1914.[5]

Historians have examined the diplomatic activity of July 1914 in minute detail. Even now in the 21st century, there is a debate as

---

5. Barbara Tuchman, *The Guns of August* (New York: The Macmillan Company 1962) 87.

to whether peace would have been possible, given skilled diplomacy and a willingness to compromise, or more ominously, whether the political and military leaders of the belligerent powers made choices they knew would lead to war.

With diplomacy unsuccessful, war fever was in the air. British Foreign Minister Edward Grey said it best while visiting with a friend on the evening of August 3rd, 1914: "The lamps are going out all over Europe, we shall not see them lit again in our lifetime." As prospects for peace dimmed, nationalism, militarism, and the alliance system lit the path to a world war.

Both the Austrian threat to Serbia and the German support for Austria caused Russia to mobilize its army to protect its Serbian ally. Russian mobilization triggered German mobilization. Together with its partners, Germany had detailed plans for fighting a two-front war against Russia to the east and France to the west.

The German war plan, or "Schlieffen Plan," created in 1905-1906, involved sending German troops through neutral Belgium to the west and into Northeastern France. Then, according to the plan, one of the German armies would go around the west side of Paris and surround the French capital city. German strategists were convinced France would fall at that point. German generals optimistically projected a 40-day war if war ever came to the Western Front.

The Schlieffen Plan also called for sending a portion of the German army east to hold off the Russians until the main enemy in the west, the French, were defeated. The Schlieffen Plan represented the best thinking of the German General staff, but some of the assumptions made did not materialize. When finally implemented in August of 1914, the plan failed.

First, the Russians mobilized more quickly than anyone had anticipated. The Germans were therefore forced to divert troops from the attack on the French and send them east to face the Rus-

"The Chain of Friendship"
Nelson Harding, *Brooklyn Eagle,*
December 4th, 1912.

sians. Second, Belgium asserted its neutrality and resented Germany for using the country as a conduit of war. Against all odds, they fought the mighty German army at the Belgian frontier. At the Fortress of Liège, Belgian forces held the German army at bay long enough to seriously disrupt the timing of the Schlieffen Plan.

Third, Great Britain joined the war. Initially, the British hesitated, but with Belgium's neutrality violated, they committed wholeheartedly to the war effort and took their place on the Western Front with the French.

A combination of factors contributed to the German failure in their initial attacks in France. Instead of going around Paris as planned, British and French forces held German armies to the east of the city. The German armies marched south and in early September were stopped at the Marne River not far east of Par-

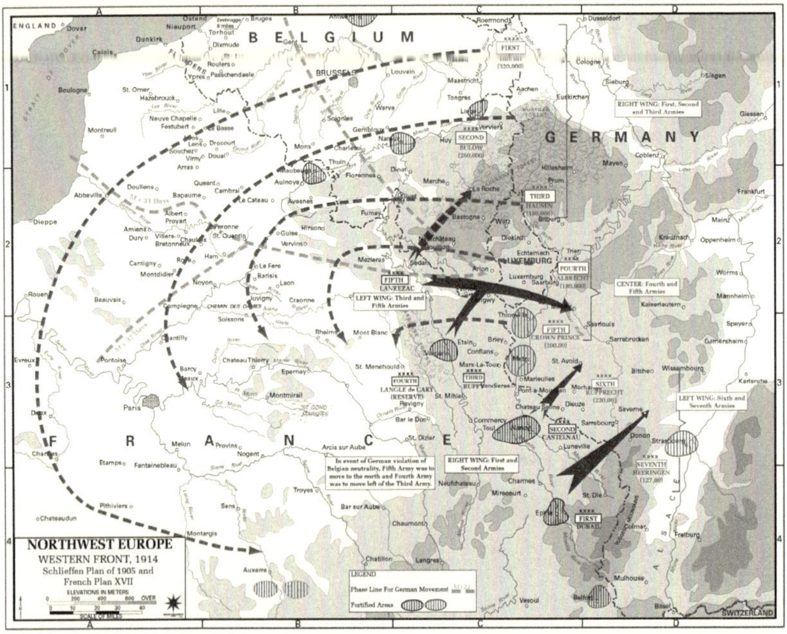

Northwest Europe, 1914, Western Front.
The Schlieffen Plan and the French Plan.
Map courtesy of the United States Military Academy Department of History.

is. After the battle at the Marne, the Germans turned and headed northeast, fighting a series of stalemated engagements until they reached the sea. At that point, both armies began digging in and creating trenches.

"War of position" replaced "war of movement." The trenches eventually reached hundreds of miles, from the northern border of France and Belgium, south to the Swiss border. The British and French established a corresponding series of trenches parallel to those of the Germans. The lines through northeast France and the northwest corner of Belgium comprised the Western front. By late 1914, the war was a defensive struggle in a bloody stalemate. "Trench warfare and static defensive lines now characterized a

German Flamethrowers in 1917.
Wikimedia Commons.

conflict previously expected to be wholly offensive in movement."[6] High explosive artillery shells and frontal assaults into hailstorms of machine gun fire generated long lists of casualties on both sides. There was no historic parallel for the losses. British planners assumed a 40% "wastage" rate over six months, but in fact losses were much higher.[7] Combat was only one of the problems. Soldiers at the front had to endure rain, snow, disease, bad sanitation, dead horses, mud, lice, and, in warm weather, a horrible stench. Life in the trenches was to say the least, an appalling experience. In the words of historian John Ellis, it was living "Eye-deep in Hell."[8]

6. Ian F.W. Becket, "The British Army and Conduct of Warfare, 1914-1918" (Seminar, MIT, October 9th, 2002).
7. Becket, "The British Army."
8. John Ellis, *Eye-deep in Hell: Trench Warfare in World War I.* (New York, Panthcon Books, 1976), front cover.

Sopwith Camel at Air Service Production Center No. 2, Romorantin Aerodrome, France, 1918.
Air Service, United States Army photograph. Wikimedia Commons.

Both sides endeavored to break the stalemate using technology. Soon after war broke out, airplanes took flight over both the Western and Eastern fronts. Used both as offensive weapons and for intelligence purposes, they proved to be a deadly new instrument of war. Beginning in early 1915, the Germans sent giant, hydrogen filled dirigibles, the "Zeps," across the North Sea, dropping bombs on targets in England. Poison gas and modern flamethrowers were particularly nasty. The flamethrowers were first used by Germany and later adopted by some, but not all, warring nations. German submarines (U-boats) attacked British warships soon after the outbreak of war, and in May 1915, the U-20 torpedoed and sank the British ocean liner *Lusitania* off the southern coast of Ireland. An estimated 1,200 civilians died, including 128 Americans. Americans responded angrily to the sinking and some wanted to enter the war, but President Wilson was able to keep the country at peace. Follow-

German Zeppelin L-13
Wikimedia Commons.

ing the American outcry about *Lusitania,* German U-boats stayed away from passenger vessels.

In 1915, Entente Powers Great Britain and France made a major effort to break the stalemate on the Western Front. The idea was a second front and their objective was the strategically important intersection of Europe and Asia, namely, the Dardanelles and Bosporus Strait which were part of the Ottoman Empire (Turkey). At the urging of Winston Churchill, First Lord of the Admiralty, the British Navy attempted to force open the water route to the Black Sea. The attack, if successful, would have made it possible for the French and British to assist the Russians who struggled on the Eastern Front. It would also relieve pressure on the Western front, hopefully breaking the stalemate there. The naval effort in February 1915 failed. However, the British and French were not ready to give up on the idea and prepared for an amphibious invasion. On April 25th, the British, together with forces from Australia and New Zealand (ANZACS), landed on the tip of the Gallipoli Peninsula at Cape Helles adjacent to the Dardanelles. The Ottoman forces were ready, losses were heavy for all combatants, and the invasion failed. After seven months of fighting, British and ANZAC forces withdrew from Gallipoli. The whole effort had been a tragic failure with heavy casualties. Over one half of the ANZAC troops sent into battle were killed.

Affairs worsened in 1916. There were three major attrition battles, two on the Western front, and one on the Eastern front. All resulted in staggering losses of human life. The plan was to wear down the enemy and destroy his means of making war.

The first of the great attrition battles in 1916 took place in eastern France near the city of Verdun. Although Verdun was not an especially strategic area during the war, it was a city with great

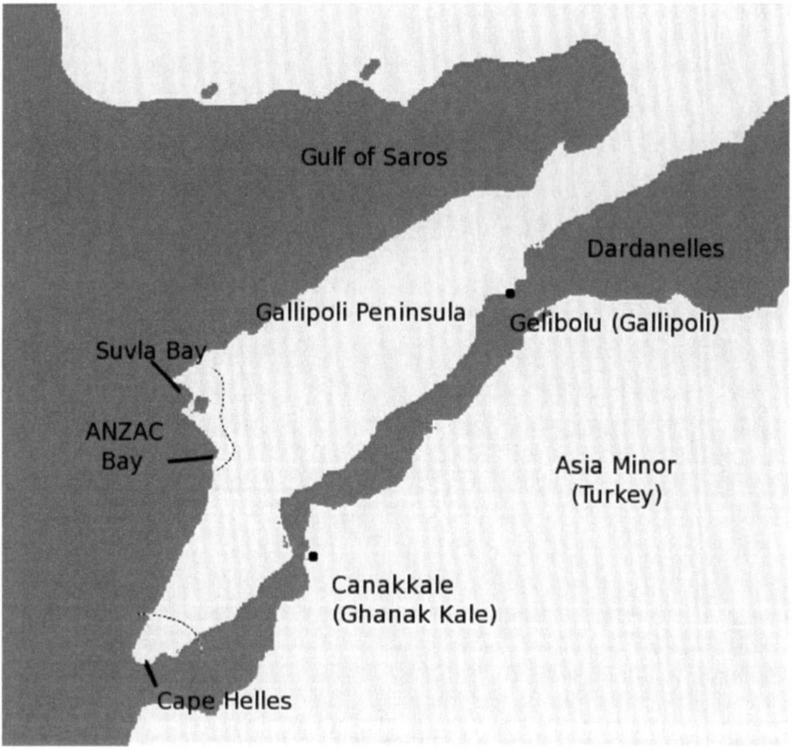

Gallipoli Map.
Public domain image.

historical significance to the French. Convinced that France would never abandon Verdun, German generals began moving troops into the area in February, 1916. The stated intention of German General Erich von Falkenhayn, Chief of The German General Staff, was to "bleed France white." He succeeded, but at great cost to Germany too. The battle at Verdun turned into a bloody slaughter. More than twenty million shells were fired into the battle zone.[9] Worse, an estimated 750,000 to 950,000 soldiers were killed or wounded in the Verdun area from February to December 1916, an astounding number on a relatively small battlefield (by comparison, U.S casualties for the entire war were about 350,000 killed, wounded and/or victims of influenza). German and French commanders continued to pour troops into the battle long after any possibility of victory had vanished. The only objective was attrition. The area became a charnel house. The millions of high explosive artillery shells churned the earth into a pockmarked hellscape. Today, segments of the battlefield remain as they were when the battle ended. The shell holes are untouched, here and there rusty barbed wire still dangles as if waiting to ensnare an unfortunate victim. Looking at it, it is difficult to imagine how anyone could have endured. Verdun was, at the time, the most expensive battle in terms of human loss in recorded history. Sadly, that level of loss and destruction would be surpassed twice more before the year was over.

The next major attrition battle of 1916 was the operation on the eastern front known as the Brusilov Offensive. Named for talented Russian General Aleksei Brusilov, the offensive operation was designed with two objectives in mind. The first objective was an effort to force Austria-Hungary out of the war. The second objective, in response to French and British urging, was an attack in the east to take

---

9. John Keegan, *The First World War* (New York: Vintage Books, 2000), 285.

pressure off the French at Verdun. Entente generals hoped the Germans would be forced to send troops east to face the Russian threat.

The offensive which began on the southeastern front, in what is today western Ukraine. Initially, it was a great success for the Russians. The offensive began on June 4th, 1916, and it turned out to be the high point of Russian involvement in the war. Throughout that summer, the Russian armies fared well, but by September 1916, all the combatants were exhausted and the offensive died out. Despite its disappointing finish, the Brusilov Offensive did achieve some of its goals. The Austro-Hungarian Army could not stop the Russians which forced German troops to be diverted from Verdun to face the threat on the Eastern front. The 1.6 million casualties in the Brusilov Offensive, were double those at Verdun.

The final of the three attrition battles of 1916 took place in northeastern France in the area of the Somme River. Like Verdun and Brusilov, losses at the Somme were astonishing. The Somme was a British and French effort to take pressure off the French at Verdun. Throughout the spring and early summer of 1916, the British prepared extensively for this major battle. Countless artillery pieces and shells were moved into the area, as well as new and relatively untested mobile weapons called "tanks." Troops moved up to the line and prepared for battle. General Douglass Haig, commander of British forces in France, was convinced that the Somme would be a turning point in the war. He believed that, with enough pressure, the British could overcome the German defenses and break the back of the German army.

The British went "over the top" at the Somme on July 1st, 1916, i.e., they left the relative safety of the trenches and attacked. In preparation for the attack, there was an extensive artillery barrage. British planners anticipated the heavy fire would destroy obstacles in no-man's land and allow troops good access to German lines.

They were wrong. The German army had dug in deep (both figuratively and literally). July 1st, 1916, was catastrophic for the British army. About 20,000 British soldiers were killed on the opening day of the battle of the Somme. At least 40,000 were wounded, and some sources put that number even higher. To make matters worse, Great Britain was using a recruiting technique called the "Pals Battalions." Young men, who were friends, neighbors, even teammates on the village football team could enlist together with the promise that they could serve in the same unit. Some "Pals" units suffered devastating casualty rates at the Somme. Villages lost many of their young men in a single day. After the Somme, most of the "Pals" were disbanded.

Throughout the summer and fall of 1916, British and French forces managed to penetrate only nine to ten miles into German held territory. When the battle was over, 1 million soldiers had been killed or wounded. Many of the dead were completely obliterated; literally nothing remained of some bodies to even bury. Today, visitors will find memorials scattered near the Somme River which contain the names of many thousands of soldiers who were never found. A century after this single battle, one can drive for miles in the beautiful Somme River valley and never be out of sight of a military cemetery.

One other major battle took place in 1916. The Battle of Jutland, on the North Sea, was the largest naval battle of World War One, and the largest naval battle in recorded history. On May 31st, 1916, the German high seas fleet left its port at Wilhelmshaven on the northern German coast and ventured into the North Sea. The German plan was to lure part of the British Grand Fleet into battle. The plan worked. The huge British Grand Fleet steamed into the North Sea from their port at Scapa Flow off the north coast of Scotland. They engaged the German fleet near the coast of Denmark, northwest of the Jutland

Peninsula. Though both countries claimed victory, the winner of the May 31 and June 1st, 1916, battle, was ultimately unclear. The British lost twice as many ships and over two times as many sailors as the Germans. When the battle ended, Britain had lost some 6,000 sailors compared to Germany's 2,500. In that sense, Germany won. However, when it was over, the German fleet steamed back to port where it remained for the rest of the war. It turned out to be the only significant surface naval battle of the war.

As an island nation, it would have been particularly devastating for Britain had the Germans prevailed. German control of the high seas would have meant no support for the British army in France because British ports would have been blockaded and Britain potentially starved out of the war.

For many Europeans, 1916 seemed endless. Families were devastated; there was never an end to the bad news. It was a pivotal year in the war.

With casualties numbering in the millions, it was becoming increasingly difficult for the governments of all warring nations to replace the losses of both men and equipment. Procuring financing for equipment, food, and servicemen was increasingly difficult. In Germany, civilian and military leaders faced increasing pressure to explain how they planned to bring the war to a successful conclusion.

While the war was terrible for all nations involved, by the end of 1916, Germany and Austria-Hungary were in an especially difficult position. One of Great Britain's first actions when the war broke out was to establish a naval blockade of Germany. With their powerful navy, it was easy for them to ensure that no significant amount of shipping could reach German ports on the North Sea. In 1914, Germany was the richest nation in Europe. With the help of fertilizer imports, the country was self-sufficient in food. With the blockade, Germany's access to fertilizer from South America, and other essential products was cut off. Furthermore, with soldiers at the front, there was a shortage of labor on German farms. From 1916 onward, it was readily apparent the blockade exacerbated Germany's substantial supply shortages and Germany faced a food crisis.

The winter of 1916-17 in Germany was known as the "turnip winter." Many civilians were malnourished, and some starved. Soldiers were not eating too well either, a shocking contrast to the prosperity of the pre-war years. Germans were angry and humiliated. German leaders, both civilian and military, were convinced that they needed to take drastic action to end the war quickly. The German government did not want to face a second turnip winter. They were not sure their nation could endure another one. For the leaders, it was a case of desperate times calling for desperate measures. They believed that ending the war in 1917 was imperative, and they were willing to take big risks to do it. However, instead of ending the war, the decisions German leaders made in early 1917 left the United States with no choice but to enter the conflict.

German U-boat UB-14
on the Black Sea 1918.
Courtesy of DeGolyer Library, Southern Methodist University.

Beginning in February 1917, Germany unleashed its fleet of U-boats. They had been used in 1915 to sink the passenger vessel *Lusitania* (discussed in chapter two). American anger caused Germany to modify the rules of engagement for the U-Boats, and the U.S. remained neutral. However, in early 1917, Germany reverted to a policy of unrestricted submarine warfare. Any ship bound for the British Isles was liable to be attacked by the deadly submarines. In practice, vessels flying the U.S. flag or the flag of any neutral nation were targets. German leaders knew such action was contrary to maritime law, but they were desperate. It was a high-risk, roll-of-the dice strategy certain to bring the United States into the war. The plan was to sink so much essential shipping bound for Britain that the British would be starved into submission before the United States could mobilize.

Throughout the winter and spring of 1917, the strategy worked. An estimated five thousand ships and millions of tons of cargo Britain could ill-afford to lose were sunk. Many ship's crews were lost too, as U-boat commanders refused to rescue them.

By May 1917, the situation was critical. Losses were far too high and essential supplies were running low. Beginning in late May, British strategists adopted the practice of assembling ships bound for Britain into convoys protected by navy warships, a strategy that proved successful. U-boats, while still deadly, could not stop enough supplies from getting to their destination to be decisive. The U-boats attacks never achieved their goal of forcing Britain out of World War One, but they played a major role in bringing America into it.

2

AMERICA GOES TO WAR

"Wilson is at heart an abject coward, or else he has a heart so cold and selfish that he is entirely willing to sacrifice the honor and interest of the country to his own political advancement."
–President Theodore Roosevelt
to son Kermit, 1915[10]

"He kept us out of war."
–Woodrow Wilson presidential campaign slogan,
1916

"They will not even come because our submarines will sink them."
–Admiral Capelle,
German Secretary of State for the Navy,
January 31st, 1917[11]

10. A. Scott Berg, *Wilson*. (New York. G.P. Putnam's Sons 2013) 378.
11. John Keegan, *The First World War*. (New York, Vintage Books 2000), 372.

> "It is a fearful thing to lead this great peaceful people into war, into the most terrible and disastrous of all wars, civilization itself seeming to be in the balance. But the right is more precious than peace, and we shall fight for the things which we have always carried nearest our hearts -- for democracy, for the right of those who submit to authority to have a voice in their own governments, for the rights and liberties of small nations, for a universal dominion of right by such a concert of free peoples as shall bring peace and safety to all nations and make the world itself at last free."
>
> —President Woodrow Wilson, "A message calling for war with the Imperial German Government in defense of American rights," April 2nd, 1917

On April 2nd, 1917, United States President Woodrow Wilson reluctantly asked Congress to declare war. Four days later, Congress responded. Both Congress and the Senate voted heavily in favor of war. After 32 months of neutrality, America was in the fight, making the conflict truly a World War.

Woodrow Wilson took the oath of office as the 28th President of the United States on March 4th, 1913. He was the first Democratic President in 20 years. At the time, most Americans thought of him as a domestic reformer. However, throughout his tenure he was forced again and again to make critical foreign policy decisions. He left office eight years later as the most influential American President ever in world affairs.

Intra-party squabbles cost Republicans the presidency in 1912. Incumbent President William Howard Taft, a conservative, received the party nomination, but at the expense of party unity. Former president Theodore Roosevelt, still popular with rank and file party members, abandoned the party, taking the Republican progressive wing along with him. Roosevelt and his supporters formed the "Progressive" or "Bull Moose" Party, a vehicle for Roosevelt to contest the election. In November, the combined vote of the two Republican groups was greater than the Democrat total. However, the split proved to be a golden opportunity for the Democrats. In the four-way contest, Woodrow Wilson, the Democratic candidate, received 42% of the popular votes, but won the electoral vote in a landslide.

As a Progressive, his campaign was based on a set of domestic reform ideas that he called "New Freedom." Antitrust regulation and more regulation of banks and business were a major part of the platform. Wilson believed the federal government should play a larger role in the economy than it had in the past.

Most of his career had been in academics as a political science and history professor. In 1902, he was appointed President of Princeton University. Politically, he was a novice. When he ran for president in 1912, 56-year-old Woodrow Wilson's political experience was limited to a single two-year term as Governor of New Jersey. He was an idealist, not always a good thing for a politician. When he was inaugurated in March of 1913, there was nothing in his background that would lead anyone to believe he would be an effective foreign policy or wartime president and he wasn't, at least not in the early years of his first term. He made some questionable decisions regarding America's relationship with Mexico, which was in political turmoil during that time. The sternest test of his idealistic leadership came in 1914 when much of Europe went to war.

How would America respond? The answer came in a message to Congress on August 19th, 1914, when Wilson articulated American policy regarding the hostilities in Europe:

> The United States must be neutral in fact, as well as in name, during these days that are to try men's souls. We must be impartial in thought, as well as action, must put a curb upon our sentiments, as well as upon every transaction that might be construed as a preference of one party to the struggle before another.[12]

As a neutral, the United States insisted upon the right to trade with all belligerent powers. Trade was important, and it meant not just goods but finance as well. Soon, American bankers were loaning millions of dollars and sending cargoes of all kinds, including weapons, to Entente Powers across the Atlantic.

However, since the Entente Powers, especially Britain, controlled the oceans of the world, the United States traded only with them. There was no other viable option. The British Navy blocked the German ports and seized American cargoes bound for Germany. That led to some tense moments in the Anglo-American relationship. The U.S. State Department protested vigorously, but to no avail. For a time, the long, friendly relationship was badly strained.

American arms sales to the Entente partners angered Germany. To stop the arms trade, German proclaimed the waters around the British Isles a "war zone" in February of 1915. All merchant vessels in those waters, including those of neutral nations, would be destroyed. The threat was real, German U-Boats were deadly, and the safety of crews could not be guaranteed.

The German policy almost forced the United States into the war following an incident on May 1st, 1915. A U.S. tanker, the *Gulflight* was torpedoed off the Cornish coast of England. *Gulflight*

12. Woodrow Wilson, *Declaration of Neutrality*, https://wwi.lib.byu.edu/index.php/President. 2020.

Drawing of the torpedoed Lusitania.
New York Herald and *London Sphere*, 1915.

did not sink, but three Americans were killed. Wilson said nothing publicly, and his advisors were divided. Robert Lansing, a State Department counselor, regarded the U-Boats as barbaric. He advocated decisive action when American rights and interests were threatened. The then-Secretary of State, William Jennings Bryan, was more conciliatory. As a pacifist, Bryan feared a sharp diplomatic exchange would rupture U.S.-German relations and lead to war. Bryan, a Midwesterner, faced heavy criticism from some prominent east coast establishment figures for his anti-war stance. President Wilson took a middle approach hoping to promote respect for United States' rights and peace.[13]

On May 7th, 1915, just a week after the *Gulflight*'s crippling, another German U-boat torpedoed and sank the British liner *RMS Lusitania* off the southern coast of Ireland. It took just a few minutes for the *Lusitania* to sink, and for 1198 passengers and crew

13. Ross Gregory, *The Origins of American Intervention in the First World War*. (New York, W.W. Norton and Company 1971), 58-59.

to perish. Among the deceased were 128 American citizens. The squabble with Britain was forgotten. Americans were outraged at what they saw as a premeditated, cold-blooded attack. The dead were non-combatants. Many were women and children. Anti-German passions were aroused.

Wilson's policy of neutrality came under fire. Former president Theodore Roosevelt, an outspoken man of action, specifically blamed the sinking of *Lusitania* on Wilson's silence after the attack on *Gulflight*. Six weeks after *Lusitania* sank, Roosevelt wrote to his son saying, "I do not believe that Wilson was right on the *Lusitania* matter. Had he acted with reasonable firmness in the *Gulflight* business the thousand men, women and children who were murdered on the *Lusitania* on the high seas would be alive today."[14]

A few days after the sinking, Wilson reiterated that America would not be drawn into the war. In his comments he used an unfortunate phrase when he said: "There is such a thing as a man being too proud to fight."[15] Exactly what he meant is not clear, but as Yale historian Charles Seymour noted, "The people of the Entente Powers were contemptuous; Germans were reassured; Americans were humiliated."[16]

After *Lusitania*, American opinion regarding the war started to change. The deliberate attack on a civilian target, especially a ship with Americans aboard, brought the war home. U.S. entry into the war, while still unlikely, was no longer unthinkable. Germany, faced with pressure from Wilson and alarmed at the prospect of America entering the fight, reigned in their U-boats. For the time

14. Theodore Roosevelt letter, http://www.shapell.org. 2015.
15. Charles Seymour, *Woodrow Wilson and the World War: A Chronicle of Our Own Times*. (New York, United States Publishers Association, Inc. 1921) 53.
16. Seymour, 53.

being, neutral ships were again off-limits. Nevertheless, there were frequent provocations as Germany tried to keep ships, even neutral vessels, from reaching Britain.

One political casualty of the *Lusitania* sinking was Secretary of State William Jennings Bryan. He disapproved of Wilson's sharp note of protest to the German government and he therefore resigned June 9th, 1915; one more casualty of the Lusitania. Few among the American establishment mourned Bryan's departure. Charles Seymour sarcastically observed, "For Bryan was willing to arbitrate even Germany's right to drown American citizens on the high seas."[17] His replacement was Robert Lansing, a talented man and unlike Bryan, a member of America's ruling elite.

As the war dragged on between 1915 and 1917, President Wilson was forced to navigate a political minefield. While the American opinion on war was starting to change, Congress and the American people were still sharply divided. Bryanites and pro-Germans, especially in the Midwest, were alarmed by and disillusioned with the prospect of America going to war.

Americans followed the events of the war daily as reporters cabled the news from Europe. The great battles of 1916 were front page news in American publications large and small. Much of what was printed came from official government sources in Paris and London. Less coverage from the German perspective was provided. The Entente partners were often portrayed as making great gains, while the "Teutons" suffered heavy casualties. Still, the accounts were relatively accurate, although specific casualty figures were rarely, if ever, disclosed. Americans were aware of what was happening, and they knew the situation in Europe was deteriorating.

Newspapers were not the only source of war information. Millions of Americans still had close connections to Europe and let-

17. Seymour, 53.

ters between friends, families, sweethearts, and others continued to make their way across the Atlantic with the latest news. There was no privacy. Sometimes the letters arrived with the notice, "opened by censor," stamped on the envelope, a sobering reminder that something was terribly amiss. Governments worried about security. The news could be grim. Sometimes they contained reports of family and friends killed or wounded. Recipients must have felt a sense of dread when they opened them.

In 1915, Elizabeth Dunn wrote from her home in rural Lincolnshire England to her son Walter, at the time a farmhand in Northern Iowa (he was soon to be a Freeborn County Minnesota farmer). "There does seem to be a lot of homes made desolate over this awful war it is just a year since it began. I wonder when it will end."[18]

On July 9th, 1916, during the battle of the Somme, Elizabeth Dunn wrote this to Walter:

> Mr. James Popples [sic] son has got killed in France. They are in trouble about it but there are thousands of parents who are in trouble at this time about their lads. My dear, I'm thankful you two are where you are at this time and not in France as you no doubt would be if you had been here when the war broke out.[19]

Elizabeth's sentiments must have been repeated in countless letters. So, despite the desire for neutrality, for many, the war was inescapable.

President Wilson sought reelection in 1916. He was opposed by Republican challenger Charles Evans Hughes. In order to run,

18. Elizabeth Dunn, *Elizabeth Dunn to Walter Dunn,* August 3rd, 1915. Dean Ulland, private collection.

19. Dunn Letters.

"Opened by Censor"
Letter from England to Freeborn County
Farmer Walter Dunn in 1918.
Dean Ulland, private collection.

Hughes resigned his seat on the United States Supreme Court. Wilson prevailed in a close vote. That Autumn, his campaign slogan was: "He kept us out of war" which proved to be highly ironic just a few months later.

As 1916 ended, the United States still maintained its policy of neutrality, but Americans were starting to sense that it might not be possible to stay that way. Even Wilson, ever the idealist, was prevaricating. In a speech in Cincinnati shortly before the election, he contradicted his own slogan when he said, "The business of neutrality is over" and that "war now has such a scale that the position of neutrals sooner or later becomes intolerable." Quoted locally on the front page of *The Daily People's Press* on October 28th, 1916, the speech was a sobering reminder of just how precarious America's situation was.

Wilson's words proved to be prophetic. He was coming ever closer to the painful decision for war. Speaking to the Senate on January 22nd, Wilson made it clear that American interests were aligned with Britain and France. Wilson admonished the British and French too, making it clear that the United States would not help them defeat Germany for their own selfish purposes. He envisioned a world without empires, where all peoples were free to determine their own government and live and work peacefully.[20] The president was starting to set forth the conditions he would later attach to U.S. entry into the war.

Events in early 1917 destroyed any hope of American neutrality. On January 31st, 1917, Germany officially unleashed its U-Boats, making war inevitable. The United States and President Wilson could not ignore the deliberate attacks on vessels which flew the stars and stripes.

On February 3rd, a German U-boat off the coast of Southwest England attacked and sank the *SS Housatonic*, a U.S. cargo vessel laden with wheat. The crew was rescued by a British ship, but the cargo was lost.

That same day, President Wilson spoke to a joint session of Congress. In his speech, he referred to the ancient friendship between "their people and our own" in the hope it could be maintained. Wilson however, left no doubt the United States would do what was necessary to protect the lives and interests of its citizens. He also announced his decision to break diplomatic relations with

20. Seymour, *Woodrow Wilson*, 104.

The Daily People's Press.

VOL. I OWATONNA, MINNESOTA, TUESDAY, FEBRUARY 13, 1917 NO. 299

Wilson Takes Firm Stand On U-Boat Policy

CLUB TO FIGHT COMMISSIONERS BUILDING PLAN

COMMERCIAL CLUB READY TO INVADE MEETING TO PREVENT BOARD FROM LETTING CONTRACT.

Signed Resolution To Be Presented

Board Plans To Open Bids On $32,-

GERMANY MUST ABAND RUTHLESS SUBMARINE WARFARÉ BEFORE UNITED STATES WILL ENTER INTO NEGOTIATIONS TO AVERT WAR

WILSON MESSAGE SENT TO BERLIN BY SWISS AMBASSADOR—LITTLE HOPEEXPRESSED THAT TEUTONS WILL MODERATE TERMS OF UNDERSEA BLOCKADE CAMPAIGN—AMERICAN RELIEF WORKERS LEAVE BELGIUM ON ORDERS FROM GERMAN GOVERNMENT — SEVENTY-TWO-AMERICANS HELD BY GERMAN GOVERNMENT WHO RESCINDS PROMISE TO RELEASE THEM.

CO-OPERATIVE ISSUES UP FOR VOTE TODAY

STOCKHOLDERS OF FARMERS' CO-OPERATIVE PACKING COMPANY WILL HOLD SESSION HERE THIS AFTERNOON.

Nine Directors To Be Elected

Fight Expected On Director In

America was moving closer to war.
The Daily People's Press, February 13th, 1917.

Germany.[21] The American ambassadors in Berlin were summoned home, and the German ambassador in Washington D.C. was ordered to leave the country.

Four days later on February 7th, the *SS California,* a British-owned liner, was sunk near the coast of Ireland with the loss of 41 lives. Now, everyone was paying attention. In February and March, the war was front page news in all the local papers. Suddenly, what had seemed so far away, came home.

U-boats were not the only issue. American public opinion was inflamed by another incident in early 1917. On January 19th, Arthur Zimmermann, a high-level aide in the German Foreign Office, sent a note to the Mexican government. Historians commonly refer to it as the "Zimmermann Telegram." In the note, Zimmermann proposed a German Mexican military alliance, with German funding for a Mexican attack on the United States. The idea was, when the war was over and the U.S. defeated, Mexico could reclaim all the territory lost to the United States in the nineteenth century. In other words, much of the American southwest.

21. Woodrow Wilson, *Address to Congress Regarding Unrestricted U-Boat Warfare,* https://www.firstworldwar.com 2020.

The Daily People's Press.

VOL. 2. OWATONNA, MINNESOTA, FRIDAY, MARCH 2, 1917. NO. 2.

KAISER PROPOSES PLOT WITH JAPAN AND MEXICO FOR WAR AGAINST U. S.

STARTLING REVELATION MADE FOR ALLIANCE ADVANCED BY GERMANY WITH TWO COUNTRIES TO FIGHT AMERICA.

COPY OF DOCUMENT IS IN HANDS OF GOVERNMENT

Details of Plot Were Left to German Minister in Mexico by Foreign Min-

MISS ELIZABETH HOY

GERMANY'S PLAN TO FORM AN ALLIANCE IS GIVEN IN DETAIL

VERBATIM COPY OF INSTRUCTIONS SENT TO MINISTER IN MEXICO TO FORM AN ALLIANCE AGAINST U. S.

EVIDENCE IS CONCLUSIVE AGAINST BERLIN OFFICIALS

Japan Was to Be Urged to Abandon Allies and Join in Attack While Mexico Was Offered Rich Rewards for Her Share of Spoils in Case of War.

BRIG. GEN. J. L. CHAMBERLAIN

CONGRESS SWINGS INTO LINE; AMAZED AT GERMAN CABAL

FORGETS DIFFERENCES OF OPINION AS RESULT OF DAY'S REVELATIONS—FILIBUSTER ABANDONED BY REPUBLICANS.

FRIENDSHIP REAFFIRMED BY JAPANESE EMBASSY

Official Comment Issued by Tokio Government—Full Confirmation of Conspiracy Given at White House—Chairman Flood Arouses Intense Enthusiasm in House.

HAPPENINGS IN CONGRESS

SENATE.

Resumed debate on revenue bill.

Military committee ordered report on army bill carrying $277,000,000.

Republican senators again threatened to tie up defense bills to force an extra session of Congress.

Passed Senate bill for prohibition in the national capital.

Sent District of Columbia appropriation bill back to conference.

HOUSE.

Passed the $129,000,000 sundry civil appropriation bill.

Foreign affairs committee considered administration resolution for arming neutral ships and appropriation for defense.

Conferees made another effort to agree on the apparently deadlocked $320,000,000 postal bill.

Prohibitionists and anti-Prohibitionists lined up for final fight over District of Columbia prohibition.

Passed administration revenue bill.

Adjourned at 12:45 a. m. (Thursday) to 12:55 a. m. Thursday.

The *Zimmermann Telegram* was front page news.
The Daily People's Press, March 2nd, 1917.

Unfortunately for the Germans, British intelligence intercepted and decoded the message. For the British, it was an intelligence bonanza and they used it to their advantage. It was released only when they calculated it would have the greatest effect on American public opinion.[22]

The Zimmermann Telegram was made public in early March. Many Americans, already angry about U-boat warfare, were enraged by the audacity of the Germans. It did not help that General Pershing and the American army had just returned from a six-month expedition in Mexico, trying in vain to capture Mexican Revolutionary leader, Pancho Villa. One year earlier, Villa and his forces raided the town of Columbus, New Mexico killing some American soldiers and civilians. About 100,000 U.S. troops were stationed on the border (many of the troops were National Guardsmen, including some from southern Minnesota). The Zimmerman Telegram exacerbated Americans' already elevated anti-Mexican and anti-German sentiment.

22. Barbara W. Tuchman, *The Zimmermann Telegram* (New York, Ballantine Books by arrangement with Macmillan Publishing Company 1985), 172-175.

"I've Had About Enough of This"
Clifford Kennedy Berryman,
Washington Evening Star, March 10th, 1916.
Berryman Collection, National Archives.

On October 8th, 1917, the *Freeborn County Standard* had this to say about America's decision for war: "It was the Zimmermann note, setting Japan and Mexico against us by promise of our dismemberment, that finally brought America into active war." The note certainly swayed public opinion, making the decision for war easier; it cannot be said, however, that there was any one single catalyst for the decision to enter the war. As for Zimmermann, who was perhaps not the brightest foreign service officer, he admitted the note was genuine, thus making it impossible for Germany to claim the incident was a setup.

Along with the U-Boats and Zimmermann, there was one other important issue looming in the spring of 1917. That issue was

"The Temptation"
Dallas Morning News, March 2nd, 1917.
Mexico was a sore spot for many Americans in 1917,
especially after the ***Zimmermann Telegram***.

money, lots of money, and much of it was owed to some of the most powerful people in America.

It has often been noted that politics and economics are inseparable. America in 1917 was no exception. Powerful people, many of them bankers, were active behind the scenes as America's leaders wrestled with questions of war and peace. Influential bankers sought to tilt American policy towards the nations that owed them money.

Throughout the war, some American banks loaned millions of dollars to the British. The capital required to carry on the war was only available through the U.S. The Morgan bank, a powerful, politically connected Wall Street institution, had a special relationship

President Woodrow Wilson asking Congress to declare war on Germany, April 2nd, 1917.
Wikimedia Commons.

with the British that went back many years. By 1917, Morgan and other Wall Street banking houses had loaned the British some four hundred million dollars (the equivalent of $10 billion dollars in 2020). U.S. banks were eager to collect. Given their immense power, no one will ever know for sure how much influence the banks had on America's entry in the war on the side of the Entente Allies.[23] Some prominent politicians, including Minnesotan Charles Lindbergh Senior, believed the banks were the deciding factor. He was outspoken in his opposition to the war (much more about Lindbergh in an upcoming chapter). Nebraska Senator George Norris was

23. Roberta A. Dayer, "Strange Bedfellows: JP Morgan & Co., Whitehall and the Wilson Administration during World War One," *Business History*, 18, no. 2 (1976).

equally blunt, warning his colleagues: "We are going to war on the command of gold."[24]

Faced with these pressures, the Wilson administration quickly discovered it was easier to talk about neutrality than to practice it. German submarines, Zimmerman, and the banks complicated everything. By early April, with all the gloomy news in the headlines, one could sense war was near. On April 2nd, President Wilson addressed Congress again, this time asking for a Declaration of War. Four days later, on April 6th, 1917, with Congressional approval, the United States of America formally entered "The Great War," World War One.

24. Ibid.

3

MINNESOTA GOES TO WAR

"There is every reason to exalt, that this land of liberty is ruled by the masterful hand of a safe and sane president, who will keep our nation neutral and who will pilot the ship of state away from the dangerous reefs of war."

–*Freeborn County Standard,* August 5th, 1914

"The war die has been cast. The United States of America is assembling its wonderful resources in the cause of freedom and against imperialism . . . There may be and is in this country a difference in opinion as to how we should enforce our demands and rights. But the great majority have decided on war as the best and quickest means to attain the goal."

–*Freeborn County Standard,* August 9th, 1917

From 1914 to 1917 the editorials in the *Freeborn County Standard* reflected the evolutionary thinking of residents throughout Minnesota. When war broke out, Minnesotans, like many Midwestern Americans, generally agreed with the Wilson administration's policy of neutrality. Most people believed a crisis in Europe should

Americans had other things on their minds in 1914. While Europe was going to war, this boy was going to the Mower County Fair.
Image made available by Daniel Cafourek.

not involve Minnesotans. Often, local newspaper editorials urged citizens to remain impartial. There was no reason to become unduly excited about events in Europe.[25]

Minnesota's ethnic make-up presented challenges to a unified war effort. In 1917, the state's population was about 2.3 million, and

25. Franklin F. Holbrook and Livia Appel, *Minnesota in the War with Germany* vol.1, St. Paul: Minnesota Historical Society, 1928, 4.

consisted of 25% native white with native white parents. Another 28% were of Scandinavian descent by birth or parentage, and 20% were German/Austrian. When American foreign policy strayed from neutrality, some (not all) Scandinavians tended to sympathize with the Germans. Minnesotans of Irish descent, while smaller in numbers, were often anti-British.[26]

Some Minnesota newspapers, such as the *Freeborn County Standard*, published news from Scandinavia in every issue, which was important for those who read only English. There were also Norwegian, Swedish, and Danish language papers available.

The German language press circulated papers to nearly 125,000 households in Minnesota. Those newspapers presented the war news from the perspective of the central powers, extolling German victories and portraying the British as the cause of the war. From their perspective, Britain was jealous of Germany's growing commercial status in the world. They pictured Germany fighting a heroic battle to avoid being crushed.[27]

Prominent individuals and organized movements were working at home and abroad for overall peace. Among them was the well-known Carnegie Endowment for International Peace. Secretary of State William Jennings Bryan, a pacifist until mid-1915, had a following in the Midwest. So too did Eugene Debs, the Socialist candidate for president in 1912, who was well known for his anti-war stance. He had a surprising amount of support in Minnesota, garnering over eight percent of the vote.

A Peace Society was formed in 1913 in Minnesota, and its membership grew. Other organizations including a Woman's Peace party joined the crusade. Even the Minnesota State Fair was involved. In 1914, the theme of Minnesota's State Fair was,

26. Holbrook and Appel, *Minnesota in the War with Germany*, 6.

27. Holbrook and Appel, *Minnesota in the War with Germany*, 7.

"Peace and Plenty," and the slogan was, "Flour barrels are better than gun barrels."[28]

Economically, Minnesota was doing well. Wartime demand for grain, meat, and butter caused farm prices to soar. By 1917, corn prices reported in local newspapers had nearly tripled what they were five years earlier. On April 7th, 1917, *The Minneapolis Morning Tribune* noted, "Sixteen-dollar hogs join two-dollar wheat"—these rates were more than double their 1914 levels. Profitable prices allowed farmers to invest in modern machinery and additional land.

High wheat prices meant high flour prices as well. The milling industry flourished. Miners on the Iron Range were busy too. In one year during the war, an incredible forty-six million tons of iron ore were shipped from Minnesota; a prodigious amount at the time.[29]

Milling, iron mining, and lumber industries provided numerous opportunities for workers, especially recent immigrants, during that period. While most Minnesotans believed that the war was deplorable, they reasoned that since they were not responsible for it, they may as well profit from it by selling all they could. As the Minneapolis Journal put it, it was "our supreme duty to feed Europe - at a price."[30]

In early 1917, events reached a climax. The German government announced the immediate resumption of unrestricted submarine warfare. President Wilson had no choice but to sever diplomatic relations with Germany. "A crisis such as one produced by American severance of relations with Germany ordinarily inflames patriotic feeling, spurs jingoistic utterance, and breeds unreasoning

28. Theodore C. Blegen, *Minnesota: A History of the State* (University of Minnesota Press, 1975), 469.
29. Blegan, *Minnesota*, 374.
30. Holbrook and Appel, *Minnesota in the War with Germany*, 6.

belligerent hysteria."[31] In Minnesota, two additional factors complicated matters. Some Minnesotans' reluctance to wage war on Germany outraged those who upheld anti-German sentiment. Additionally, radicalism was a concern. A militant labor union known as the International Workers of the World (the IWW) were antiwar, as were socialists. Minnesota congressman Charles Lindbergh and other non-socialists such as Wisconsin Senator Robert La Follette questioned President Wilson's actions regarding Germany. Senator La Follette stated that he would not follow the president under all circumstances. Socialist Minneapolis mayor Thomas Van Lear made a similar public pronouncement.

Soon, however, people who saw themselves as patriots began to view questioning or opposing war as synonymous with treason. Mayor Van Lear was roundly criticized in the pages of the *Minneapolis Tribune* for his refusal to blindly follow the president. Pro-and anti-Wilson gatherings were held. In Minneapolis, a loyalty league was founded. Minnesotans were sharply divided.[32]

During this chaotic period, the Minnesota legislature still met in regular session. Naturally, the legislature had ordinary business to attend to. But, in response to the war fever sweeping the state and the nation, the legislature enacted what may well be the most controversial piece of legislation ever in the history of the state of Minnesota.

On April 17th, 1917, eleven days after the formal declaration of war, Governor J.A.A. Burnquist signed legislation establishing the Minnesota Commission of Public Safety. The intent of the legislation was to create a governing body that could efficiently mobilize the state's resources and people. The Commission was given wide

31. Carl H. Chrislock, *The Progressive Era in Minnesota 1899-1918,* Minnesota Historical Society Press, 1971, 130.

32. Chrislock, *Progressive,* 131.

ranging powers and was essentially a dictatorship. The Commissioners, appointed by Burnquist who served as its chairman, was given the power:

> To do all acts and things non-inconsistent with the Constitution or laws of Minnesota or of the United States which, in the event of war existed between the United States and any foreign nation, are necessary and proper for the public safety and for the protection of life and public property, or private property requiring protection; and all acts and things necessary or proper so that the military, civil and industrial resources of the state may be most efficiently applied towards maintenance of the defense of the state and nation, and towards the successful prosecution of such war.[33]

The Commission held its first meeting on April 23rd, 1917. From that day on, it was busy directing the war effort in Minnesota. In its efforts to promote loyalty, patriotism, and efficiency in the state, the civil liberties of individual Minnesotans were often ignored. The Commission was, in the words of University of Minnesota History Professor Hy Berman, "A reign of terror that wiped out civil liberties, wiped out freedom of expression, wiped out freedom of association . . . that created a kind of climate where, in fact, it ruled by force."[34]

The wide range of the Commission's activities were aston-

---

33. J.A.A. Burnquist et al. *Report of Minnesota Commission of Public Safety*, St. Paul: Louis P. Dow Co.
34. Hy Berman, "Spies, armed militia, and suspended civil rights in WW1 Minnesota" https://www.mprnews.org/story/2017/04/06/.

ishing. Fifty-nine orders were issued dealing with a wide variety of issues. For example, milk and bread prices were regulated and orders were issued regulating or suppressing the liquor trade in Minnesota. Aliens were required to register. The registration form included 35 questions and their property rights were regulated. All able-bodied men living in Minnesota were required to find employment. The Commission even established a forest fire relief fund.[35]

Few aspects of life in Minnesota escaped the Commission's attention. The minutes of the Commission's meetings show that it investigated and commented on a wide variety of other issues. For example, resolutions were issued regarding the coal supply, food, union problems, farm labor, soldier's welfare, and the Home Guard. The Nonpartisan League (NPL) was investigated for what the Commission termed "seditious activities." It even investigated the use of German language textbooks in Minnesota schools. It proclaimed English as the official language and even went so far as to issue a blacklist of German books that should not be used in schools. There seemed to be no end to its ability to reach into the affairs of Minnesotans.[36]

Perhaps the most infamous incident in the Commission's history involved the Brown County seat of New Ulm. In 1917, many New Ulm citizens were ethnic Germans. Eight to ten thousand people gathered in New Ulm on July 25th, 1917, to protest the draft. The demonstrators argued that draftees should not be sent beyond America's borders. "The speakers urged compliance with the law, but challenged the justice of the war . . . "[37] The mayor presided over the demonstration, and other city officials participated. To the

35. J.A.A. Burnquist et al. *Report.*

36. J.A.A. Burnquist et al. *Report.*

37. Paul Nelson, "New Ulm Military Draft meeting 1917" MNOPEDIA, January 11th, 2016, https://www.mnopedia.org.

The Commission had a role in everything, even propaganda.

Blooming Prairie Times, April 11th, 1918.

Commission, the city officials' participation smacked of disloyalty and they began an investigation. After a lengthy hearing process in which the New Ulm officials proclaimed their loyalty and patriotism, Governor Burnquist removed the duly elected city attorney and mayor of New Ulm from office. One of the speakers that day, Albert Steinhauser, an outspoken New Ulm lawyer and newspaper publisher was arrested and charged with the federal crime of sedition (he was never prosecuted).[38] The incident was not yet over. In 1918, the Minnesota Bar Association revoked the membership of the city attorney. No draft refusal took place in New Ulm, citizens did their duty, and the mayor and city attorney returned to office after the war. The incident demonstrates the power of the Commission during the war.

The Commission's work was always intended to benefit the people of Minnesota and the United States during a period of crisis. For the most part, it did. However, the Commission had few legal checks to its power and serious abuses occurred that would not have happened under ordinary circumstances.

38. Ibid.

4

CALL TO ARMS

"Be sure of your date of birth.
June 5 is registration day."
–*Freeborn County Standard,* May 24th, 1917

"Sheriff issues warning to obey registration law–Register June 5."
–*The People's Press,* May 28th, 1917

"Mower County registered more than the government estimated as her quota last Tuesday. There were no slackers here."
–*Mower County Transcript-Republican,*
June 13th, 1917

"OFF TO SUMMER HOME IN SOUTH CAROLINA: After a Brief Sojourn Will Tour France, Belgium and Germany to Look for the Kaiser's Goat."
–*Mower County Transcript-Republican,*
July 31st, 1918

"A farewell party was held at the Torkel Aldahl farm near Corning last Sunday in honor of Marbo Aldahl, Edward Basness, and Carl Tverberg who will leave for training camps this week. About 150 friends were present."

Blooming Prairie Times, July 25th, 1918

The great decisions had been made. In Washington, Congress and the President set America on a course for war. In St. Paul, Minnesota, the Governor and Legislature did their part by creating the Minnesota Commission of Public Safety and passing other wartime legislation. Now it was up to the people: those who would feed the nation, pay for the war, and support the effort in countless ways. First, however, America needed a much larger military. It was up to the many young men who would have to fight.

In 1917, the American military establishment was tiny. There were about 127,000 troops in the United States Army and 14,000 officers and men in the Marine Corps. By comparison, Germany had 11 million, and France had 8 million. Obviously, American forces were not substantial enough for such a large undertaking as a world war. The government used three approaches to find the additional manpower it needed to engage enemies in Europe and at sea.

First, mobilizing the National Guard with its dual role was the fastest way to raise military forces. Nationwide, there were about 180,000 men in Guard units. In April 1917, the Minnesota National Guard, a force of some 7,500 men, was composed of three infantry regiments and a small naval militia. Because of repeated border violations and tension with Mexico, the infantry units did have some limited experience. President Wilson federalized many state guard units, including some in Minnesota for service on the U.S. Mexican border. Called up in June of 1916, the First Minnesota

Infantry was sent to southern New Mexico for border duty. The experience was something of a debacle. Like most states, the Minnesota guard contingent proved to be undermanned, with some units existing only on paper. Austin-based Company G sent 100 men to New Mexico in 1916, but a year later their enlisted numbers had fallen to 60. Furthermore, many of the Minnesota troops lacked the necessary training and equipment to be effective. To make matters worse, some officers were political appointees and not fit for military duty.

Following the United States' diplomatic break with Germany in February of 1917, the Minnesota Guard began taking measures to increase their numbers and readiness. Recruiting efforts were increased throughout the state. Posters, speakers, newspaper advertisements, and slide presentations in theaters were used to recruit more Minnesota guardsmen. The effort was somewhat successful. By April of 1917, the total force had increased, but the number of guardsmen remained relatively small. Recruiting was a tough sell. At first, there was a long six-year enlistment and it was impossible to explain exactly what the Guard's role would be.

After the declaration of war, in order to enhance effectiveness and readiness, the Minnesota Guard was reorganized. The 2nd Infantry Regiment, representing southern Minnesota, was headquartered in the Rice County city of Faribault. Company locations were established in 12 cities, from Worthington to Winona, including Austin and Owatonna. In 1917, Austin's G Company had been continually in service for 35 years. Along with other southern Minnesota guardsmen, they played an important role during the war. However, their numbers were small, and America's needs were great. Other means would have to be found to provide the necessary manpower.

Company G, Minnesota National Guard on Main Street in Austin, MN, just before deployment to Camp Cody in New Mexico.
Mower County Transcript-Republican,
April 17th, 1918.

The second method used to increase America's fighting capability was to encourage volunteers. This method was used throughout the war. President Wilson aspired to build the military totally with volunteers, and while there were some, numbers were far less than what was required. Despite Wilson's encouragement, Americans did not rush to enlist. In the first six weeks after the declaration, only 73,000 volunteered.[39] In Minnesota, the situation was somewhat different. During the war, some 40,000 Minnesota men enlisted in the various branches of the military.[40] Given Minnesota's population of 2.3 million, that was a significant number.

---

39. Howard Zinn, *A People's History of the United States:1492-Present* (New York: Perennial Classics, 1999), 364.
40. Blegan, Minnesota: *A History of the State*, 474.

"Red Blooded Men" 1917 Recruiting Poster
focused on southern Minnesota.
Minnesota Historical Society.

That left the third method, conscription. Wilson said as much in his War Message to Congress:

> It will involve the immediate addition to the armed forces of the United States already provided for by law in case of war at least 500,000 men, who should, in my opinion, be chosen upon the princi-

> ple of universal liability to service, and also the authorization of subsequent additional increments of equal force so soon as they may be needed and can be handled in training.[41]

He recommended the immediate addition of 500,000 men to U.S. fighting forces and more when they "may be needed and can be handled in training." Faced with the disappointing lack of volunteers following American entry, conscription turned out to be the only way to raise such large numbers of men.

To address the problem, Congress passed the Selective Service Act on May 18th, 1917. The Act authorized the President, albeit temporarily, to increase the size of the armed forces as needed. Eligibility for the draft was determined by age, gender, marital status, and number of underage dependents in the family. In all, there were five classes of conscription candidates. Class 1 was composed of healthy single men, aged 21-30. They were first in line for the draft. Classes 2-5 were those who were married, the sole support of their families, some government officials, pilots, clergy, and felons. Men from classes 2-5 were deferred until such time as the class 1 cohort was exhausted (and in fact, no one was ever drafted from classes 2-5). Local draft boards were organized to classify the registrants. Appointed by President Wilson, the local boards were often comprised of county officials. Board members' names were well known, there were numerous reports of their activities in area newspapers.

In Steele County for example, Sheriff Leahy, Auditor Parcher, and County Physician Dr. C. Peterson made up the board. In Freeborn County, the board was composed of Dr. C.F. Calhoun, Peter Fosse, and Fred Davis. N.E. Peterson was the appeal agent.

41. Woodrow Wilson, "War message to Congress" (speech, Washington D.C., April 2nd, 1917), https://wwi.lib.byu.edu. 2020

The blindfolded Secretary of War Newton D. Baker drew the first number (258) in the draft lottery on July 20th, 1917.
Public domain image.

In Mower County, draft board members were Sheriff Nicholson, Dr. Lewis (also director of public health), and Dr. Pierson. Each county draft board had members in every township and village, as well as in all the city precincts. The draft boards also contained a medical advisory committee, examining doctors, and a legal advisory board. In Freeborn County, the Selective Service Organization had 122 members, not including administrative staff.[42] The draft process required a substantial bureaucracy; it was a big job. The boards were responsible for the registration process, organizing the registration cards, and making some determinations regarding exemptions. For example, local boards could exempt registrants who

42. C.E. Wood compiler, *In the World War 1917-1918-1919: Freeborn County Minnesota*, (Albert Lea Minnesota: Albert Lea Publishing Company, 1919).

failed their physical examination. Other exemptions, like requests to stay home and help on the farm, were determined by the regional draft board in Mankato. The regional boards also heard appeals. Moral/religious objections and employment in an essential area of the economy (like agriculture or a war related industry) were also grounds for possible exemption.

The army was not prepared for a sudden influx of men. Training camps, equipment, and uniforms were all in short supply. It was therefore necessary to implement a fair method to determine who among the eligible draftees went first. The federal government went to great pains to create an equitable plan for mobilizing the draftees. The order in which eligible registrants would be called was determined by a draft lottery.

The Selective Service Act contained two important caveats designed to make American fighting forces representative of the nation. First, based on lessons learned during the Civil War, no one could avoid conscription by hiring a substitute, meaning affluent Americans could not escape service. Second, unlike the practice in the Spanish-American War, high profile individuals could not raise their own private forces without presidential authorization. Much to the disappointment of former President Theodore Roosevelt who dreamed of a new force of "Rough Riders," President Wilson made no such authorizations.

June 5th, 1917, was the first of what would eventually be three registration days. Every man in the United States between the ages of 21 and 30 was required to register, except for National Guard members and those already enlisted. Illness was no excuse. Those unable to register for themselves were required to send an agent to do it for them.

Registration was so important that Minnesota Governor Burnquist ordered all Minnesota saloons closed for the day. Worried

COUNTY QUIET WHEN YOUNG MEN GO TO REGISTER

PROSPECTIVE SOLDIERS OBEY LAW WITH ALACRITY—ALL NATIONALITIES ENROLL FOR ARMY.

Heavy Registration In Owatonna

Reports From County Indicate Day Was Peaceful—Tramps Appear To Follow Letter of Law.

Without a hint of disorder or trouble, Steele county's young men, subject to military duty, registered at their voting precincts, Tuesday.

All Nationalities There.

All nationalities thronged to the registrars' tables, answered the twelve questions asked on the cards and went their way. Reports that reached Sheriff Leehy from all registration places, indicated that America's prospective soldiers were complying with the law to the letter.

All Obey Law.

"I have not heard of any cases where men between the ages of 21 and 30 years, inclusive, have failed to register," Sheriff Leehy said Tuesday night shortly after 9:30 o'clock when all registration places had closed and the registrars and clerks were busy tabulating the answers.

No draft day incidents in Steele County.
The Daily People's Press, June 6th, 1917.

about anti-draft activities, media outlets ensured the penalties for refusing were heavily publicized. "Registration must be made today, or the U.S. will prosecute" read a grim headline in the June 5th, 1917, *Owatonna People's Press*. The paper went on to warn that "for the sake of your own liberty, don't let anybody talk you out of registering. The penalty for failure to register is sure and severe." Registration went on without disruption in Steele County.

Freeborn County made the day a patriotic holiday. It "was made the occasion of a celebration such as will always be remem-

Freeborn County Standard.

MINNESOTA HISTORICAL SOCIETY

VOL. 62, No. 11 ALBERT LEA, MINNESOTA, MONDAY, JUNE 4, 1917 Established 1857

ALL HONOR TO THE BOYS WHO REGISTER

FIERCE FIGHTING MARKS ACTIONS IN TWO BIG SECTORS

BRITISH AND GERMANS MAKE GAINS IN ARRAS AND LENS TERRITORY BUT ARE UNABLE TO HOLD ALL.

FRENCH INFLICT BIG LOSS ON TEUTONS

FIFTEEN FROM TWIN LAKES

ALL HONOR TO YOUNG MEN WHO WILL REGISTER

CLAIMED HOLIDAY BY MAYOR WOHLHUTER FOR CELEBRATION OF EVENT.

PARADES, MUSIC AND SPEECHES ON BIG PROGRAM

BUSINESS MEN LAUNCH LIBERTY LOAN CAMPAIGN

FREEBORN COUNTY AND ALBERT LEA ASKED TO SUBSCRIBE FOR $400,000 WORTH OF BONDS.

THEO. SPELTZ ELECTED TO HEAD LOCAL DRIVE

RUSSIA REACHED BY U. S. MISSION HEADED BY ROOT

AMERICAN ENVOYS ARRIVE AT SLAV PORT AFTER FAST TRIP ACROSS PACIFIC ON NAVAL VESSEL.

UNSTINTED AID READY FOR NEEDY COUNTRY

"ALL HONOR TO THE BOYS WHO REGISTER"
Freeborn County Standard, June 4th, 1917.

bered by the large number who participated. If any Albert Lea people were absent it must have been because of total disability."[43]

As one might imagine, the process of registering and classifying the men was complex. Requests for deferment had to be considered based on the classification system mandated by Congress. The process was explained in detail by the authors of the Freeborn County history entitled, In the *World War 1917-1918-1919 Freeborn County Minnesota,* written shortly after the armistice. The registration form was two pages long, and a legal advisory board helped ensure the accuracy of the registration. The men were required to provide information concerning their age, occupation, dependents, marital status, birthplace, citizenship status, and health. Usually, requests for deferment were made because of family dependence

43. C.E. Wood compiler, *In the World War 1917-1918-1919: Freeborn County.*

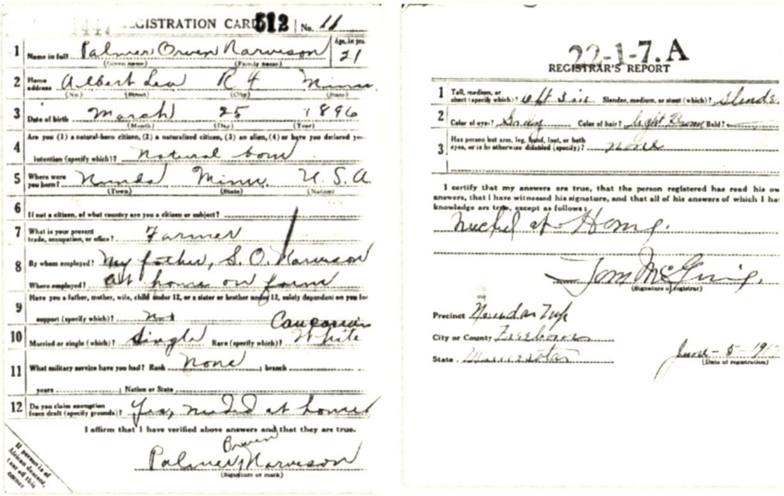
REGISTRATION CARD 512 No. 11

1 Name in full Palmer Owen Narveson Age, in yrs. 21

2 Home address Albert Lea R 4 Minn

3 Date of birth March 25 1896

4 Are you (1) a natural-born citizen, (2) a naturalized citizen, (3) an alien, (4) or have you declared your intention (specify which)? natural born

5 Where were you born? Nunda Minn. U. S. A

6 If not a citizen, of what country are you a citizen or subject?

7 What is your present trade, occupation, or office? Farmer

8 By whom employed? my father, S. O. Narveson Where employed? at home on farm

9 Have you a father, mother, wife, child under 12, or a sister or brother under 12, solely dependent on you for support (specify which)? Not

10 Married or single (which)? Single Race (specify which)? Caucasian White

11 What military service have you had? Rank none; branch; years; Nation or State

12 Do you claim exemption from draft (specify grounds)? Yes, needed at home

I affirm that I have verified above answers and that they are true.

Palmer Owen Narveson (Signature or mark)

22-1-7.A

REGISTRAR'S REPORT

1 Tall, medium, or short (specify which)? 6 ft 3 in. Slender, medium, or stout (which)? Slender

2 Color of eyes? Gray Color of hair? Light Brown Bald?

3 Has person lost arm, leg, hand, foot, or both eyes, or is he otherwise disabled (specify)? none

I certify that my answers are true, that the person registered has read his own answers, that I have witnessed his signature, and that all of his answers of which I have knowledge are true, except as follows:

Needed at Home.

Tom McGuire (Signature of Registrar)

Precinct Nunda Twp

City or County Freeborn

State Minnesota June 5 1917 (Date of registration)

Note the Registrar's statement on the second page.

Palmer Narveson's draft registration card. Freeborn County, Minnesota. *Ancestry.com.* http://www.ancestry.com : 2020.

or occupation. Those engaged in agriculture and industrial production were sometimes deferred because of their importance to the national economy. Those requests were forwarded to a district board headquartered in Mankato. Local newspapers were asked to remind readers that local boards had nothing to do with agricultural exemptions. This reminder appeared in the *Mower County Transcript-Republican* on January 23rd, 1918, which read "If you are seeking exemption on account of agriculture, don't bother the local draft board for it has nothing to do with this class of exemptions. If it is your only reason for exemption you are put in class A. The district board at Mankato considers all agricultural claims. (County papers please copy.)"

A look at draft registration records indicates that young men who sought deferment so they could stay home and help on the

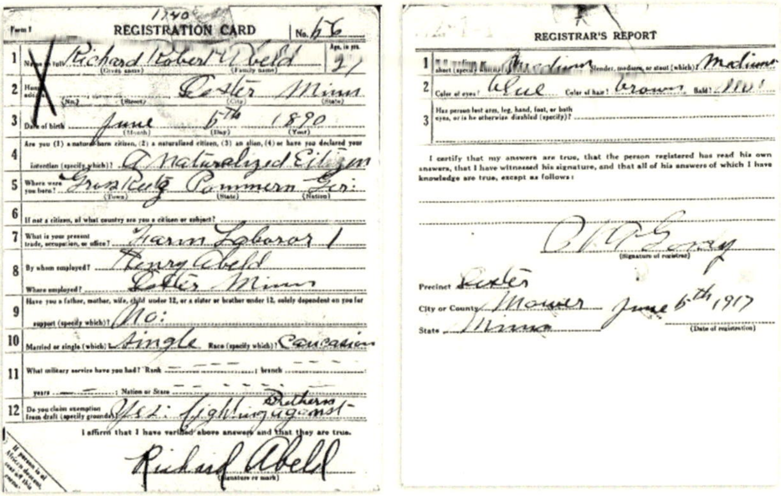
1740

Form 1 REGISTRATION CARD No. 66

1 Name in full Richard Robert Abeld (Given name) (Family name) Age, in yrs. 27

2 Home address Dexter Minn (No.) (Street) (City) (State)

3 Date of birth June 6th 1890 (Month) (Day) (Year)

4 Are you (1) a natural-born citizen, (2) a naturalized citizen, (3) an alien, (4) or have you declared your intention (specify which)? A Naturalized Citizen

5 Where were you born? Gross Reetz Pommern Ger: (Town) (State) (Nation)

6 If not a citizen, of what country are you a citizen or subject?

7 What is your present trade, occupation, or office? Farm Laborer

8 By whom employed? Henry Abeld
Where employed? Dexter Minn

9 Have you a father, mother, wife, child under 12, or a sister or brother under 12, solely dependent on you for support (specify which)? No:

10 Married or single (which)? Single Race (specify which)? Caucasian

11 What military service have you had? Rank — branch —
years —; Nation or State —

12 Do you claim exemption from draft (specify grounds)? Yes: fighting against brothers

I affirm that I have verified above answers and that they are true.

Richard Abeld (Signature or mark)

If person is of African descent, tear off this corner.

REGISTRAR'S REPORT

1 Tall, medium, or short (specify which)? Medium Slender, medium, or stout (which)? Medium

2 Color of eyes? Blue Color of hair? Brown Bald? No!

3 Has person lost arm, leg, hand, foot, or both eyes, or is he otherwise disabled (specify)?

I certify that my answers are true, that the person registered has read his own answers, that I have witnessed his signature, and that all of his answers of which I have knowledge are true, except as follows:

(Signature of registrar)

Precinct Dexter
City or County Mower June 6th 1917
State Minn (Date of registration)

"Yes: fighting against brothers," line 12.
Richard Abeld's draft registration card.
Mower County, Minnesota. *Ancestry.co*m.
http://www.ancestry.com : 2020.

farm were often denied. One such example includes young Palmer O. Narveson, a Nunda Township, Freeborn County farmer who claimed a farm exemption on his registration card. The township registrar, Tom McGrif, refused to certify that he was needed at home.

There were some especially poignant requests. Mower County resident, Richard Robert Abeld, a 27-year-old Dexter area farm laborer claimed exemption because, as he described it, he would be, "fighting against brothers." Abeld was a naturalized citizen, born in Gross Reetz Pomerania, a German province, in 1890. His request was denied, and he entered service in Austin during September of 1918. He never went overseas, so the nightmare of fighting his brothers did not come to pass. He was discharged in January of 1919.

It was not just farmers' sons who were denied exemptions. When twenty-five-year-old Jay C. Hormel, Vice-President of the George A. Hormel Company, registered in Austin, he claimed his

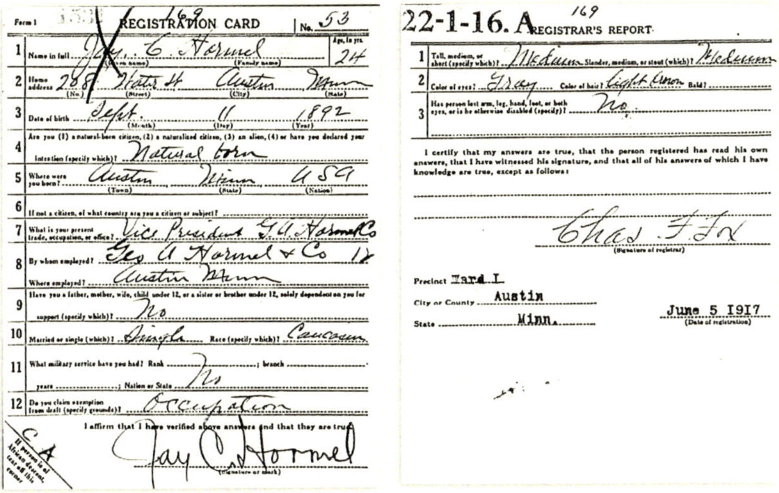

Form 1 REGISTRATION CARD 169 No. 53

1 Name in full Jay C. Hormel (Given name) (Family name) Age, in yrs. 24

2 Home address 288 Water St Austin Minn (No.) (Street) (City) (State)

3 Date of birth Sept. 11 1892 (Month) (Day) (Year)

4 Are you (1) a natural-born citizen, (2) a naturalized citizen, (3) an alien, (4) or have you declared your intention (specify which)? Natural born

5 Where were you born? Austin Minn USA (Town) (State) (Nation)

6 If not a citizen, of what country are you a citizen or subject?

7 What is your present trade, occupation, or office? Vice President G.A. Hormel Co

8 By whom employed? Geo A Hormel & Co 17
Where employed? Austin Minn

9 Have you a father, mother, wife, child under 12, or a sister or brother under 12, solely dependent on you for support (specify which)? No

10 Married or single (which)? Single Race (specify which)? Caucasian

11 What military service have you had? Rank ; branch years ; Nation or State No

12 Do you claim exemption from draft (specify grounds)? Occupation

I affirm that I have verified above answers and that they are true.

Jay C. Hormel (Signature or mark)

If person is of African descent, tear off this corner.

C A

22-1-16. A 169 REGISTRAR'S REPORT

1 Tall, medium, or short (specify which)? Medium Slender, medium, or stout (which)? Medium

2 Color of eyes? Gray Color of hair? Light brown Bald?

3 Has person lost arm, leg, hand, foot, or both eyes, or is he otherwise disabled (specify)? No

I certify that my answers are true, that the person registered has read his own answers, that I have witnessed his signature, and that all of his answers of which I have knowledge are true, except as follows:

Chas F. Fox (Signature of registrar)

Precinct Ward I
City or County Austin
State Minn.

June 5 1917 (Date of registration)

Jay Hormel's draft registration card.
Mower County, Minnesota.
Ancestry.com.
http://www.ancestry.com : 2020.

occupation as the basis for an exemption. The request was denied, and he entered service as a private in September of 1917. Like Narveson and many other local men, Jay Hormel served with distinction, he was discharged a First Lieutenant in December of 1918.

The following list shows the numbers in the order in which they were drawn. The first number in each case represents the order in which the second, or red-ink registry, number was taken from the bowl. Four numbers are given in each line. Beginning with the first number, which was drawn by Secretary Baker.

1—258	2—2522	3—9613	4—4532
5—10218	6—458	7—2403	8—10015
9—9899	10—8934	11—1438	12—2624
13—4762	14—854	15—6985	16—7183
17—6597	18—5977	19—1894	20—4614
21—4501	22—9922	23—1878	24—4142
25—4083	26—10425	27—9018	28—8251
29—6423	30—9136	31—1257	32—6799
33—10240	34—6767	35—1095	36—8668
37—2022	38—3383	39—6551	40—6952
41—9420	42—3382	43—9258	44—4306
45—4320	46—7103	47—9652	48—4881
49—1453	50—3679	51—6183	52—3755
53—783	54—1813	55—8462	56—2787
57—1858	58—8239	59—2389	60—10388
61—5034	62—7269	63—8904	64—5706
65—3567	66—3637	67—9938	68—5227
69—1752	70—5497	71—8836	72—8596
73—4520	74—2494	75—6463	76—4137
77—5885	78—3674	79—5939	80—5769
81—3200	82—3082	83—6131	84—6909
85—3505	86—1117	87—8343	88—1572
89—5897	90—2762	91—9594	92—1748
93—5938	94—7953	95—9316	96—2195
97—4487	98—8159	99—839	100—5019
101—9369	102—7730	103—2036	104—8671
105—5997	106—7376	107—10254	108—337
109—6810	110—676	111—6446	112—6768
113—7355	114—275	115—6047	116—6833
117—6259	118—9985	119—4410	120—3827
121—509	122—1185	123—564	124—4056
125—10088	126—5637	127—2166	128—945
129—1913	130—8806	131—10496	132—596
133—10070	134—5980	135—2543	136—5830
137—3067	138—2620	139—2936	140—9309
141—1267	142—4433	143—3746	144—5510
145—2148	146—536	147—3812	148—1495
149—2453	150—7191	151—3640	152—10098
153—10242	154—7753	155—548	156—128
157—3070	158—7319	159—7025	160—9149
161—1679	162—5678	163—9453	164—3604
165—8331	166—7719	167—1237	168—784

893—3556	894—6292	895—4666	896—2778
897—81	898—10188	899—9725	900—9986
901—4768	902—1432	903—9152	904—6481
905—7331	906—1727	907—2047	908—3595
909—3711	910—3230	911—8936	912—8448
913—10289	914—2817	915—7377	916—8419
917—7523	918—7801	919—10010	920—7823
921—4764	922—4893	923—2740	924—8722
925—981	926—7566	927—1848	928—1044
929—6145	930—3376	931—8795	932—9695
933—6902	934—7935	935—9444	936—5364
937—5456	938—7467	939—9211	940—5802
941—6843	942—4588	943—4977	944—2662
945—8147	946—4987	947—10341	948—9095
949—1570	950—5120	951—3932	952—2884
953—2885	954—1817	955—2577	956—770
957—8263	958—882	959—10406	960—6535
961—10131	962—8741	963—8900	964—1004[illegible]
965—4123	966—3570	967—2078	968—7616
969—6910	970—677	971—8912	972—2119
973—2360	974—5439	975—9739	976—749
977—8516	978—8221	979—4281	980—2269
981—9390	982—7260	983—3304	984—8805
985—3450	986—6261	987—8797	988—6272
989—8200	990—6868	991—4646	992—2592
993—6680	994—8260	995—8132	996—7235
997—3736	998—7553	999—2758	1000—6570
1001—6282	1002—1868	1003—1509	1004—7676
1005—3836	1006—1211	1007—7704	1008—9338
1009—4131	1010—525	1011—3342	1012—1417
1013—9207	1014—1574	1015—2034	1016—7291
1017—8853	1018—2434	1019—10374	1020—8488
1021—5110	1022—9241	1023—10102	1024—9073
1025—3770	1026—3087	1027—760	1028—6463
1029—4641	1030—183	1031—7363	1032—3435
1033—56	1034—2695	1035—8965	1036—4061
1037—1276	1038—9999	1039—7831	1040—6403
1041—4476	1042—8961	1043—3685	1044—7067
1045—1791	1046—1956	1047—792	1048—2128
1049—7313	1050—9427	1051—3612	1052—4798
1053—3311	1054—6590	1055—4139	1056—3692
1057—6724	1058—7209	1059—5251	1060—7551
1061—8889	1062—6818	1063—3469	1064—8747
1065—7357	1066—3059	1067—9776	1068—7740
1069—7573	1070—4550	1071—6707	1072—5
1073—350	1074—10054	1075—10413	1076—1580
1077—10271	1078—54	1079—2698	1080—728
1081—7060	1082—2365	1083—3831	1084—7726
1085—10194	1086—2615	1087—870	1088—5922
1089—1714	1090—8242	1091—4533	1092—5975
1093—549	1094—1132	1095—7430	1096—440
1097—1485	1098—5926	1099—1674	1100—741
1101—8875	1102—1054	1103—9058	1104—2836
1105—9878	1106—1275	1107—8499	1108—2316
1109—8341	1110—3160	1111—7347	1112—9581
1113—7826	1114—4752	1115—3334	1116—8477
1117—2225	1118—10260	1119—711	1120—1022
1121—7629	1122—5941	1123—7261	1124—841
1125—8586	1126—10176	1127—6938	1128—3502
1129—638	1130—4244	1131—7237	1132—9170
1133—6788	1134—6246	1135—2795	1136—6090
1127—4673	1138—8405	1139—2454	1140—8687
1141—5634	1142—1032	1143—8634	1144—[illegible]

A partial list of call-up numbers from the complete list published in the Ellendale Eagle. Most newspapers published the numbers. Men of service age were called up according to numbers drawn in Washington D.C.

Ellendale Eagle, July 26th, 1917.

n, $1.50 per year. SOCIETY OFFICIAL COUNTY PAPER

DRAFT BOARD IS BUSY EXAMINING REGISTRANTS

Several Rejected and Many Others File Exemption Claims on Account of Dependents or Otherwise.

The county examining board for the selective army have been as busy as bees the past few days examining those in the first call. We were not able to get complete information and details for this issue but submit a list of those who failed to pass the physical test and those who passed the physical examination and filed affidavits for exemption an account of dependents, or otherwise:

REJECTED

1095—Frank J. Klempe, Waltham
1752—Elmer C. Jacobson, Austin
1813—Earl J. Oudseck
1858—Stanley E. Thompson
509—Edward M. Schammel
596—Geo. M. Baarsch, Spring Val.
1267—Louis A. Huseby, Adams
2148—Myron R. Vaughn, Austin
548—Ben Holgate, Austin
1679—Michael F. Dugan, Austin
107—Leo Remer, Toapi
1563—Robert Madden, Austin
616—Leonard Mantel, Spring Val.
1891—Chris. D. Anderson, Austin
1986—Archie W. Hazeltine
1539—Joseph E. Jones, Austin
309—Peter B. Benson, Ostrander
437—Otto F. Schulze, Elkton
1324—Thorman O Lund, Lyle
1264—Michael Gilgenbach, Adams
1178—James A. Storry, Lansing
[illegible]—Conrad N. Peterson, Lyle

604—P. S. Hawkins, Spring Valley
1763—Chester Kellner, Austin
1548—Chas. M. Lerach, Austin
1014—Sander E. Edgar, Sargeant
514—John Till, Rose Creek
433—Carl Qualey, Adams
10—Ole E. Eng, LeRoy
487—Thomas J. Majerus, Rose Crk.
1323—Emil Lunderblade, Lyle
1487—Harry J. Smith, Austin
1536—Lawrence B. Jensen, Austin
432—Louis H. Peterson, Rose Creek
18—Martin J. Hatletredt, LeRoy
927—Geo. J. Lawsen, Racine
1322—Louis E. Larsein, Lyle
1103—Henry Ruliter, Brownsdale
1771—Howard H. Kramer, Austin
1020—A. G. Gronsetti, Sargeant
1651—Glenn A. Burroughs, Austin
1955—Melvin R. Erickson, Austin
223—J. P. Murphy, R6, Austin
390—Erick E. Severside, Taopi
75—Everett T. Goble, Taopi

Draft registrants in the left column failed their physicals, those on the right claimed an exemption. They were called based on the number to the left of their names.
Mower-County Transcript-Republican, August 15th, 1917.

5

OVER THERE

"The glamour and romance of war appeal to a youngster of 18 . . . until he tries it."[44]

"We are getting hardtack and canned horse to eat."[45]

"The best thing to do is lie flat
on the ground and pray."
–Letter from Claude Christgau to his sister,
Mower County Transcript-Republican,
December 11th, 1918

"Joseph Pirkl killed in action: First Steele County
boy dies on the battlefield."
–*Blooming Prairie Times,*
July 25th, 1918

44. Wilbur Peterson, *I Went to War,* (Marshall Minnesota: The Messenger Press, 1938).
45. Walter Hartmann Unpublished Diary, 1918, Mower County Historical Society.

> "Otto Thompson Lund, son of Mr. and Mrs. Chris Lund was killed in action in France August 2nd. His parents received a telegram Tuesday afternoon announcing his death. He was in the United States regular army in which he had enlisted and served about two years. The Lund family have the sympathy of all in their bereavement."
>
> –*Owatonna People's Press*, August 30, 1918

In 1918, the war got personal. It was not just training for the young American soldiers, it was real. Wilbur Peterson found this out, as did Claude Christgau, Walter Hartman and many others. During the war, Austin native Walter Hartman wrote a diary. Twenty years after the war, Marshall native Wilbur Peterson published a memoir. Both were excellent writers, both were straightforward about their experiences, and neither were censored. They are excellent southern Minnesota sources for "unvarnished" information.

As the men were sent to fight, the Western Union messages families dreaded started to arrive. "The Secretary of War desires me to express his deep regret . . . " Soon the sad notices appeared in the newspapers. The Lund family of Blooming Prairie was not alone in their sorrow.

With training camps up and running by late 1917 and throughout 1918, American troops poured into France. At war's end, more than 2,000,000 young Americans were serving there in some capacity. Hundreds of them were from southern Minnesota. It seemed every country's soldier had at least one nickname, some of them unprintable. American troops were "Doughboys," or "Sammies." There are theories as to the origin of the American nicknames, but no certainty. About half of the Americans were combat troops, the rest worked in support roles behind the lines. There were also local men in the Navy.

Women volunteers, though smaller in number, also played a vital role in the war effort. Women were not drafted, but some young women enlisted, at least eight of whom were from Mower County. [46]Four Freeborn County women served in the American Nurse Corps and five as Red Cross nurses. Women volunteers and enlisters were at risk just like their male counterparts. Nurse Effie Alinda Larson from Clark's Grove died after contracting influenza and pneumonia at camp Dodge.[47]

Some women served overseas in the Red Cross, YMCA, and other organizations. Exact numbers are difficult to ascertain, but their contributions in administration and nursing were essential to the success of American forces. Many young servicemen owed their lives to the dedication of American nurses.

Everyone who served reacted differently to their wartime experience. Some came home and never talked about it. They wanted to forget the things they had seen and done, and for them it was best to leave the memories alone. On the other hand, some found solace and kinship in sharing their experiences. The parts they played in the war have been handed down to us in the form of memoirs, diaries, letters, and of course in the stories they told to family and friends. These accounts are priceless. They tell us about what they had to endure, what it was like to be a soldier, sailor, or nurse at that time. However, the letters were censored. Soldiers were not allowed to use much detail, and it's likely many of them wanted to avoid worrying their families. Therefore, they are often vague

46. Nicholsen, et al. *Mower County in the World War* John H. and Gertrude E. Skinner eds. (Austin Minnesota: Austin Herald, 1919), 157.

47. C.E. Wood compiler, *In the World War 1917-1918-1919: Freeborn County Minnesota*.

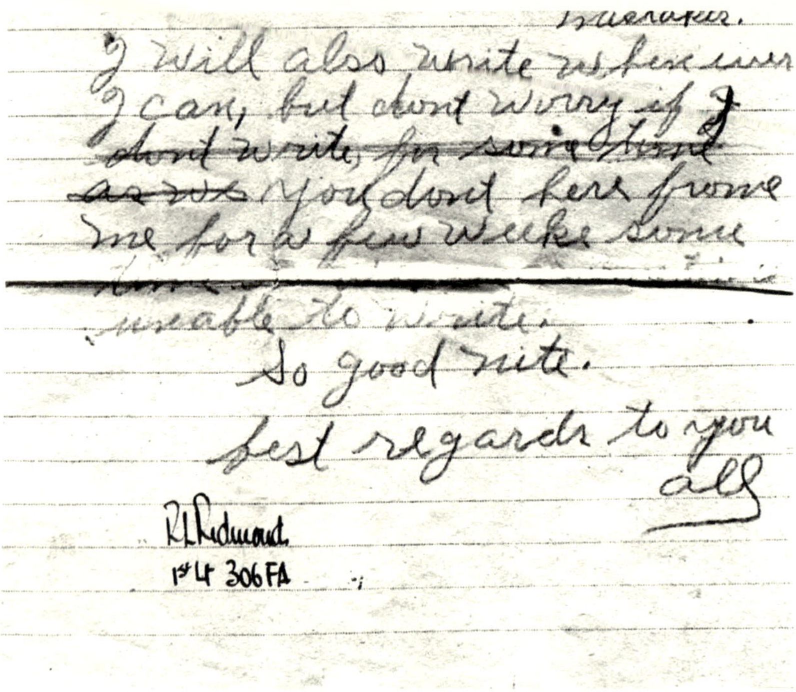

I will also write whenever
I can, but dont worry if I
dont write, for some time
as soon you dont here frome
me for a few weeks some
[illegible] [illegible]
unable to write.
So good nite.
Best regards to you
all

R L Redmond
1st Lt 306 FA

Steele County soldier Herman Grunklee's letter from August 18th, 1918. Note the censor's signature.
Steele County Historical Society.

about some of the details. Weather, crops, people and scenery are the usual topics, not much about battle or life at the front. One of the duties of low-ranking officers was to read the letters and delete sensitive information before they were mailed. It is common to see the initials of a Lieutenant at the end of letters from France.

Culture shock was a common theme. Paris, and the battlefields of France are a long way from southern Minnesota, and many of the young Americans had never been far from home. The things they saw, sometimes on duty as a soldier, sometimes on leave as a tourist, were almost beyond belief. Many letters mention the contrast to Minnesota, especially its age. The sites ranged from ancient, picturesque villages, still quite primitive to Americans accustomed to modern life in America, all the way to beautiful French châteaux.

Herman Grunklee's letters are an example. Grunklee, a Steele County man farming with his father before being drafted, opened his letters home with the heading "somewhere in France." Along with the usual comments about the weather, he was concerned with the farm and family back home. In an August 1918 letter home, he remarked " . . . going to church is something I can't do here which disappoints me very much for I miss it." Herman was in the 306th field artillery. He received his training at Camp Dodge, and in France. Part of his job was caring for horses. The 306th was involved in heavy fighting, yet the only thing Herman had to say about it was, "For as we are camping in the woods and everything is quite unhandy."[48] In one October letter, he did refer to the front as "not a very nice place to be."[49]

Then there were the temptations of city life: the wine, women, and song. American Doughboys' pay went a long way in wartime France. It was easy to get into trouble. In the words of the popular vaudeville tune, "How ya gonna keep 'em down on the farm after they've seen Paree?" In fact, it wasn't just "Paree." Writing about Liverpool, England in his diary, Walter Hartman of Austin commented, "The girls are plentiful here."[50]

Usually, letters home did not mention the seamier aspects of the soldier's experience, but the U.S. government was concerned. Unlike their European allies, American leaders, perhaps mindful of their constituents back home, expected the troops to sublimate their natural impulses and remain celibate. They were worried

48. Letter from Herman Grunklee to his family, August 18th, 1918. Steele County Historical Society.

49. Hermann Grunklee to family, October 7th, 1918.

50. Hartmann, Diary.

about the impact of French sexual mores on members of the American Expeditionary Forces (AEF). A massive educational campaign launched to warn soldiers about the dangers of venereal disease. "A central theme of the campaign was: better dead than diseased."[51] With slogans like: "A German bullet is cleaner than a whore."[52] The message was blunt. We are left to imagine the reactions of rural Minnesota soldiers.

Everyone suffered from fear, loneliness, and sometimes boredom, but beyond that there was no universal experience. The individual narratives are unique.

France and the battlefields lay across the Atlantic 4,000 miles away from Minnesota. The first step was getting there, and sometimes the journey itself proved to be an adventure. After the stateside portion of a "Doughboy's" training was complete, it was time to move out. The first segment for most soldiers was a long, crowded rail journey from the training camps to an East Coast transient depot where they waited for a troopship. For many soldiers, the destination was Camp Merritt in New Jersey, near the New Jersey Port of Hoboken. Others went to Camp Upton on Long Island while they waited to embark. Walter Hartman, who was bound for Hoboken from Camp Lewis in Washington, generally enjoyed the trip across the country. The scenery was interesting, and everyone had plenty to eat and smoke. Still, it was occasionally uncomfortable. He recalled a stop along the way in Minnesota, and swimming in a river near Montevideo. His comment, " . . . surely enjoyed it. We where [sic] dirty as hogs."[53]

---

51. Allan M. Brandt *No Magic Bullet: A Social History of Venereal Disease in the United States Since 1880* (Oxford: Oxford University Press, 1987), 101.
52. Ibid.
53. Hartman, Diary.

Herman Grunklee, a rural Steele County soldier in the 306th field artillery, enjoyed most of the trip from Camp Dodge to Camp Upton. Along the way his unit stopped in New York City. He was amazed. "But say you ought to get in the city of New York that is something that opens a fellows [sic] eyes."[54]

Finally, oftentimes after a long wait at the port, the recruits were crammed aboard troopships bound for Europe. Some stopped in England first, others went directly to France.

Ironically, thousands of American troops were transported aboard vessels seized from Germany. For obvious reasons, the captured German steamer *President Lincoln* kept its name. Blooming Prairie area soldier Alvin Lysne and Marshall native Wilber Peterson, were crammed aboard *President Lincoln* (six months before it was torpedoed) along with 6,000 other soldiers on an October-November 1917 passage to the French port of St. Nazaire. Peterson had a way with words, and in his memoir, he described the voyage like this:

> Oh for the roominess of a thickly packed sardine!
>
> Thirteen days of it. Days with endless monotony. Days of torpedo scares. Days when the ship seemed to drop beneath us as the engines stopped to fool wary submarine ears. Days of seasickness, when soldiers' faces turned a pasty green. Days of target practice. Days of band concerts, and boxing, and singing. Days of fear when ships scurried around in circles and oil and wreckage slipped by.
>
> Thirteen nights of it. Nights of freezing sleep. Nights

54. Herman Grunklee to his family, March 29th, 1918.

> of maddening heat in the Gulf stream. Nights filled with smelly seasickness . . . A couple of dozen life-boats, two or three score rafts. For six thousand men! Filth and rotten odors everywhere. No such thing as a bath . . . And those life preservers! Black from soot, and stinky from spilled food.
> "No feeding the fishes over the rail either." Barrels on deck for that. Filth? Plenty!
>
> Cables flash the word back: "S.S. President Lincoln arrived St. Nazaire"- and in New York, the mail trains leave with six thousand postcards, written and left there before sailing, bearing the words to as many homes, "Arrived safely over there."[55]

Wilbur Peterson both traveled to France on the *President Lincoln* (not on the same voyage). In a letter published in the *Blooming Prairie Times* on November 7th, 1918, Lysne commented: "I came over on the *President Lincoln.* It was torpedoed on the way back to the states, 24 hours after we were off from it. They did not bother us coming over however. We were well protected from attack. We had 16 ships, two of them battleships, ten destroyers and four transports. We even had some airplanes the last days."

Another torpedo attack cost Albert Lea native Leo Martin Carey his life. Carey, a Navy Radio Operator aboard the *U.S.S. Tyler* delivering wheat to Genoa, Italy, was killed when the ship was torpedoed May 2nd, 1918. Carey stayed at his post and went down with the ship. [56]

---

55. Peterson, *I Went to War,* 4.
56. C. E. Wood, *In the World War: 1917-1918-1919 Freeborn County Minnesota,* (Albert Lea Minnesota: Albert Lea Publishing, 1919).

The Freeborn County Standard's front-page report on Carey, May 9th, 1918, didn't mince words: "Carey is the first local victim of the ruthless Hun warfare."

Usually, captured German vessels were given new names. The American ships *Agamemnon (Kaiser Wilhelm II), Von Steuben (Kronprinz Wilhelm)* and *Leviathan (Vaterland)* all began their lives as German ocean liners. "Queer tricks war plays - the *Vaterland,* made by the enemy, now carrying troops to fight her native land."[57]

Once the troops were underway, the U-Boat threat was on everyone's mind. Memories of the British liner *Lusitania,* torpedoed off the Irish coast in 1915 with heavy loss of life, were still fresh. The United States and British navies went to great lengths to protect the troopships. Beginning in May 1917, all allied ships bound for Europe traveled in convoys with naval destroyer escorts, zig-zagging their way across the ocean.

Blooming Prairie native Helmer Kaatrud served on a navy submarine chaser that protected allied shipping. Shortly after the war was over, he described the process of attacking the U-Boats in a letter to his sister. The letter was published in The *Blooming Prairie Times* on January 2nd, 1919. It must have escaped the censor's attention since it provides a lot of detail about chaser operations. Three ships worked together, in wireless communication with each other. They had both short-and long-range devices for detecting the subs. Kaatrud himself must have worked below deck, writing, "its [sic] hell to be an engineer" with all engines running at full speed in pursuit of "Fritz." Smoke and heat made the engine room a miserable place to be. When they found him, "Fritz" must have been terrified. "Well we have a thing that looks like an ash pan which contains 300 pounds of the strongest explosive. Believe me, it will jar him up when it gets near him. When we roll one out and it ex-

57. Peterson, *I Went to War,* 1.

plodes underwater it lifts our boat out of the water. Not saying what it would do under pressure." Kaatrud concluded his description with evident satisfaction, writing, "It will blow him to hell."

The U-Boats sank thousands of ships, but the escorts, manned by sailors like Kaatrud, as well as the advent of the convoy system in mid-1917, significantly lowered shipping losses. Other than *President Lincoln,* few U.S. troopships were hit.

Walter Hartman, aboard the British Steamer *Armagh* bound for Liverpool, described the embarkation in his diary.

> July-7 Left Port at 6:30 A.M. and (illegible) at Sandy Hook until our convoy was collected. Saw the Statue of Liberty. Fourteen transports, 2 destroyers, 1 cruiser and 2 airaplanes [sic] accompained [sic] us the first day out. Sure is a wonderful sight to see ships all in formation.

Hartman also described conditions aboard, "Very crowded and the smell is worse. But we are soldiers and not supposed to crab."[58]

While the convoy system made the crossing safer, the practice of zigzagging to avoid attack proved to be hazardous on at least one occasion. In a November 1917 incident, the USS *Von Steuben,* bound for the French port of Brest with the Sixth Marine Regiment aboard, was involved in a mid-Atlantic collision with the Agamemnon, another American troopship. Both ships were damaged, but temporary repairs at sea kept them afloat. They arrived safely in Brest on November 12th. Young LaCrosse Wisconsin native, Myron Herreid, a marine aboard the Von Steuben described the collision:

58. Hartmann, Diary, 3.

> The *Agamemnon* came up abreast of us and turned towards us hitting our bow with her side. The shock was quite severe, and this was followed by a second one as our boat swung against the Agamemnon smashing all our lifeboats which hung over the starboard side. Those on the other ship started to scream when they saw the collision was inevitable. We heeled over to the port side on the impact, and then the collision sirens sounded.[59]

James Hatcher, another Marine on the *Von Steuben* had this to say:

> At the moment of impact, I felt a shudder run the length of the *Von Steuben*, then the *Agamemnon* rolled against us. Side to side, amid the noise of rasping steel and the shouts of men, the *Agamemnon* rolled over us until she seemed almost directly above us and our decks almost vertical. All hands made their way quickly to their appointed stations and made ready to 'abandon ship.' The *Von Steuben* began to list to starboard almost immediately and in short order she lay at a very unpleasant angle. But the gobs [sic] were quickly on the job and worked frantically to repair the damage.[60]

Fortunately, both vessels made it to port. One adventure over, they began training for another.

---

59. Myron Herreid Unpublished Diary, November 9th, 1917. Rick Herreid, private collection.
60. James Hatcher Unpublished Memoir, Rick Herreid, private collection.

Usually, the voyage across did not involve a mid-ocean collision. It was miserable but not especially dangerous. The peril was more imagined than real. Ships did collide, and U-Boats were a threat, but those incidents were rare. The most common complaints were about the crowded conditions, the stink, and seasickness aboard the transports.

Most soldiers made the trip successfully. By April 1918, some 12,000-15,000 men were landing in France nearly every other day:[61] tired, hungry, smelly, some still queasy from seasickness, and most of them curious about the Old World.

For Herreid, Peterson, Hartman, and virtually all recruits, there was still more training required. The Americans were unfamiliar with the British and French weapons they would use. Consequently, the Allied Expeditionary Force established a large training facility near Verdun, scene of the horrible 1916 battle, but for the time being a relatively quiet area. Doughboys worked with the new weapons and trained in the tactics they would employ at the front. Drills, hikes, and exhaustion were all part of the training routine. So, too, was griping about the food. In a letter to his mother in Owatonna written shortly after the war ended, private O. V. Partridge was blunt: "The mess Sergeant is a fine fellow so 'they' say [they meaning the old men from Calif.] but I'm damn sure he missed his calling."[62] Troops spent a lot of their pay on treats like chocolate and jam, sometimes complaining about prices charged by the French. When they could find it, rabbit, purchased from the French, was on the menu. High priced or not, Walter Hartman really enjoyed

61. Joseph E. Persico, *11th Month 11th day 11th Hour Armistice Day, 1918: World War I and its Violent Climax*, (New York: Random House, 2004), 225.

62. Letter from O.V. Partridge to his mother, January 1919. Steele County Historical Society.

rabbit.[63] Letters and food boxes from home were cause for celebration. Foods did survive the long journey from America; they may have been stale, but they were a taste of home for lonely soldiers.

Occasionally, soldiers were able to find some humor in their situation. In a letter home published by the *Blooming Prairie Times* on November 14th, 1918, Blooming Prairie area resident Hans O. Kirkeby facetiously noted just how tough soldiers' lives were, especially regarding their tobacco supply. "We get all the Bull Durham we want, but no Copenhagen, that alone makes me mad enough to kill every Boche in front of me so I can get to where there is some Copenhagen." ("Boche," pronounced "bowsh" was a derogatory slang term for German soldiers). Kirkeby also noted that he still couldn't "parlez vous" but he was learning.

Jokes aside, tobacco really was important. In his memoir, Canadian soldier Harold R. Peat noted: "Candies, cigarettes and ordinary, plane [sic] cigarettes are good enough, so long as you send plenty. If he chews, send him chewing. Cigarettes are an absolute necessity because they are the only thing soothing through the nerves when under heavy shellfire."[64]

For the most part, Americans did not go into battle for more than a year after the formal U.S. declaration. There was some small scale participation in late 1917, but at the time there were not enough trained U.S. soldiers in France to make a difference. By May of 1918, AEF Commanding General Pershing had several divisions of trained troops (a U.S. infantry division at full strength was 28,000 men),[65] with more being added every day. He was satisfied that his men were prepared to fight effectively, so American

63. Hartman, Diary.

64. Harold R. Peat, *Private Peat*, (New York: Gosset & Dunlap, 1917,) 234.

65. "US Army Divisions in The Great War" *Global Security*, accessed October 27th, 2020. https://www.globalsecurity.org.

units began to deploy near the front.

Despite General Pershing's desire for complete control of all U.S. troops, the first units were placed under British or French command. Total American command would come later. However, Pershing insisted on Americans fighting together. Despite repeated requests, they were never fed into the lines as replacements for decimated French and British companies. The U.S. high command was not impressed with their allies' tactics. In their view, years of trench warfare and senseless frontal attacks had wasted countless lives. Americans would not fight that way.

When they were ready, the Americans fought valiantly. The contributions the AEF made in the fierce fighting from May to November 1918 tipped the balance. Some historians believe that the AEF won the war.[66] The Germans and their allies could not hold out against a seemingly endless stream of fresh, well-fed, and well-equipped American troops, some of them young men from southern Minnesota.

In 1918, Americans fought in many places across a long and shifting front. The first Freeborn County soldier killed in action was nineteen-year-old Vernon Bailey who was from the village of Freeborn in the northwestern part of the county. Bailey entered service as a volunteer on May 9th, 1917, before Congress passed the Selective Service Act. He shipped out to France in June of 1917 after only two months of training. He was in the 16th Infantry, AEF, a part of

66. Geoffrey Wawro, *Sons of Freedom: The Forgotten American Soldiers Who Defeated Germany in World War One,* (New York: Basic Books, 2018), 8.

* It was the 16th that marched in Paris on July 4th, 1917, to bolster French morale. They stopped at Lafayette's tomb where Lieutenant Colonel Charles Stanton is said to have proclaimed "Lafayette we are here!"

the First Expeditionary Division, one of the first American units to enter the fight.* The First soon became famous as the "Big Red One" (named after its distinctive shoulder patch). Sent to the Picardy sector in northern France to relieve exhausted French troops, Bailey and his company were in the trenches five days without rest. On May 11th, 1918, with his unit short on food and water, Bailey and three others volunteered to get supplies. He was killed by shrapnel in the attempt. Bailey was interred at Broyes, France.[67] *The Freeborn County Standard* described him as a "fine boy of good habits and character." His bright future was gone.

Nearly two weeks later, the first major AEF offensive took place on the River Somme near the French village of Cantigny. The result was an American victory; the village was captured along with many German soldiers. As important World War One battles go, it was small, but for inexperienced American troops it was important. The price was high, with over 300 killed, and 1,600 total casualties, but the Doughboys acquitted themselves well, doing what they had set out to do. The fight instilled a sense of confidence in American fighting ability.

Twenty-year U.S. army veteran, and Freeborn County resident Sergeant John O. Frydenlund fought at Cantigny. He was in Company C, 28th infantry, also a part of "The Big Red One." On the front line continuously for nearly two months, Frydenlund was killed in action on July 21.[68]

Cantigny was the only the beginning. The AEF faced much worse over the next 167 days. The next battles were farther south, near the River Marne, to the east of Paris, and they proved to be a baptism by fire for thousands of young Americans.

Before the war turned it to rubble, Chateau-Thierry was a bus-

67. Wood, *In the World War: Freeborn County.*

68. Ibid.

tling French city. Lively sidewalk cafes lined the River Marne with a not-to-distant air of romanticism. Not far to the west lay Belleau Wood, a wealthy Frenchman's hunting preserve. Today, the Wood looks much as it did a century ago: a small forest, quite beautiful from a distance. Today, its foliage still hides crumbling trenches, gun emplacements and rusted ammunition. The lush fields of wheat on its perimeter sway gently in the breeze, but they too have something to hide. After all these years, the earth beneath them is still infested with countless pieces of once deadly shrapnel. Wilbur Peterson called the stuff "spare parts." "They tear your flesh for near the ultimate in ugliness and pain . . . "[69]

The battles at Cantigny, Chateau-Thierry, and Belleau Wood were part of Germany's last desperate gamble to win the war known as "Operation Michael," or the "Kaiserschlacht" (Kaiser's Battle). With Lenin and the Bolsheviks in power, Russia was out of the war. A treaty with Germany in March formalized the matter in the east, simplifying the situation for German High Command. With just one front to contend with and troops that were trained in new tactics named for German General Oscar von Hutier, their war effort was reinvigorated. On March 21st, 1918, Germany launched attacks along the length of the Western Front.

The Paris-Metz road, an important route into Paris, lay to the city's east along the River Marne. It was on the southern sector of the front and both sides knew control of the road was critical. German access to Paris would have been a disaster and may have ended the war. The stakes were high as the Germans pushed south. It was essential to stop them before they seized the road.

Chateau-Thierry, astride the River Marne and along the road, fell to the Germans on June 1st, 1918. From there, the German army moved west, taking control of Belleau Wood. Every step of their

69. Peterson, *I Went to War*, 51

The wheatfield at Belleau Wood in 2015. In 1918, U.S. marines advanced to the Wood through this field. Many were "harvested" by German machine guns.
Photo courtesy of Karen Herreid.

advance brought them closer to controlling the entire road. The opposing French and British troops were exhausted, spread too thin to protect the road. American troops were sent in to help stop the surging Germans. This is Wilbur Peterson's recollection of the place: "Chateau Thierry--drop in your tracks at night, wake up surrounded by dead men and swollen horses. The flies, the stench. The stench, it still nauseates us until we sweat."[70]

The U.S. 2nd Division, a hybrid unit including a brigade of Marines as well as army troops, advanced a few miles west of Chateau Thierry near a small woods about one mile long and a quarter mile wide known as "Belleau Wood." After a long, forced march,

70. Ibid., 10.

they succeeded in plugging a hole in the line left open by worn-out French troops. The Americans, fighting as a unit but under overall French command, stood in front of Belleau Wood between the Germans and the Paris-Metz road. German forces continually strengthened their positions in the Wood. Their gun emplacements and trenches inside the Wood made it a formidable, deadly obstacle. Nevertheless, U.S. commanders were determined to push the Germans out. The marines proved up to the task. It took 26 days of bitter, bloody fighting, some of it by frontal attacks across open wheat fields, to drive the Germans from the Wood, but they did it. In the process, the farmland and nearby villages were devastated. The Americans proved to be ferocious fighters. They advanced, facing artillery barrages, machine guns, even hand to hand combat.

It was tough going, but they persevered. The road was safe. The battle took a grim toll. The AEF suffered about 10,000 casualties (killed or wounded), including over 1,800 killed. The German body count is unknown, although it must have been high. Wilbur Peterson had this to say about Belleau Wood:

> A highway. Paris to Metz. A significant beauty still, but the old trees paralleling its sides are reduced to ragged stumps, by shellfire. Trees that grew for half a century after God made them-until man came along in his fury.
>
> A wheat field. The grain is sparse and trampled. Men have moved through it--and now there's many a rifle standing butt end up, bayonet in the ground. Each marks a soldier harvested by the machine guns concealed in the wood just ahead.[71]

71. Ibid., 27.

Belleau Wood was a searing experience for the raw American forces. The fighting was brutal, much of it at close range in dense woods. When it was over, everyone knew the AEF (especially the Marines) could fight. The French renamed Belleau Wood "The Wood of the Marine Brigade."[72] Even the Germans, who had earlier denigrated the American fighting abilities, were impressed. There are stories, perhaps apocryphal, of German soldiers calling the Marines "Teufel Hunden" or "Hellhounds." AEF Commander Pershing remarked afterwards, "The deadliest weapon in the world is a United States Marine and his rifle."[73] Belleau is also where Gunnery Sergeant Dan Daly, leading his platoon into the German machine guns, is said to have shouted "Come on you sons of bitches! Do you want to live forever!?[74] To this day, Belleau Wood has a special place in the lore of the United States Marine Corps.

Some young Minnesota men fought at Belleau Wood, and some died. Charles Harcourt Earl, 19 years old and a Corporal in the 6th Marines, was killed at Belleau Wood on June 16th, 1918. Earl, born in Moscow Township, Freeborn County, and a resident of Austin, dropped out of Austin High School as a senior to enlist in the Marines. An ambitious young man, he delivered the *Herald*, was employed by Decker Hardware, and even worked for the Post Office. At the 1917 AHS Commencement ceremonies, "his chair was vacant, and his diploma left in the empty seat." The account went on to note that "Charles Earl was the first of the boys who enlisted in his country's service to fall."[75]

---

72. American Battle Monuments Commission, 2020, www.ambc.gov.
73. John J. Pershing "Belleau Wood," *Marines*, October 27th, 2020, https://www.6thmarines.marines.mil.
74. SSgt Dieter Stenger "The German Defensive Plan at Belleau Wood," *Doughboy Center*, November 1st, 2020, http://www.worldwar1.com.
75. Nicholsen, *Mower County in the World War*, 7-17.

The Aisne-Marne American Cemetery near Belleau Wood. Many of the U.S. and French soldiers who were killed at Belleau wood and Chateau-Thierry are buried there.
Photo Credit: Warrick Page/American Battle Monuments Commission.

Loren Hervey Woodle, an Austin native, Austin High School graduate, and university student also enlisted in the Marines in April 1917. His story is a sad one. A qualified sharpshooter, Woodle was wounded at Chateau-Thierry on June 5th, 1918. Initially, he was treated at hospitals in France. Later, he was transferred to the naval hospital in Portsmouth Virginia. In late 1918 or January 1919, his parents traveled to Portsmouth and accompanied Loren to the naval hospital at Lyons Colorado. On January 10, 1919, Mrs. Woodle wrote a touching letter to Loren's friend and fellow Austin High School graduate Alex Hirsh. One can sense a mother's hope in her comments: "We are hoping he will get well here altho [sic] the Drs. at Portsmouth did not give us much encouragement."

Mrs. Woodle also stated that Loren wasn't strong enough, so she was writing his letters for him. She closed with a plea to Alex: "Write Loren as often as you can."[76] Loren died in Colorado on February 24th, 1919. [77]

Freeborn County soldier, Sergeant Arthur Everett Nelson was killed in action July 2nd, 1918, near Vaux. A small northeastern French village, not far from Chateau-Thierry, Vaux was the scene of heavy fighting in early July. Nelson, sick at the time, "moved forward under intense shelling to maintain communication with an attacking battalion of the infantry and was killed in this heroic action." He was awarded the Distinguished Service Cross. [78]

Charles Burton, from Pleasant Valley Township in eastern Mower County, fought at Chateau-Thierry. He survived, only to be shellshocked at Verdun in the autumn. Burton died in February 1919.

The fighting, death, and destruction continued through the summer. The Germans, as always, fought hard, but were continually pushed back. Joint Franco-American operations stopped German forces and defeated them both at Chateau-Thierry and farther north in the Soissons area. Casualties were heavy. The Germans had no choice but to pull back all along the front. Although any hope of seizing the strategic Paris-Metz road was gone, the fighting and dying continued. By late July, Germany's Operation Michael was a spent force.

The church bells tolled in Blooming Prairie for Otto Lund, who was killed August 2nd, 1918, just a few days short of his nineteenth birthday. Lund was the first to fall from the Steele County community. He was born in Denmark and had a unique story. According to *The Blooming Prairie Times*, he enlisted before his seventeenth

---

76. Mrs. C.F. Woodle to Alex Hisch, January 10, 1919, in Hirsch Letters, Mower County Historical Society.
77. Nicholsen, *Mower County in the World War*, 7-17.
78. Wood, *In the World War: Freeborn County*.

birthday and had a natural aptitude for military affairs. He came down with pneumonia and was discharged. When fully recovered, Lund enlisted again, this time in the Minnesota National Guard, Steele County's Company One. There he became a sharpshooter. Well known for his mechanical ability, *The Times* reported that he was supposedly killed while driving a tank.

Lund wasn't the only local soldier to die fighting in a modern machine of war. Lieutenant Lee C. Prentice was a Fairmont resident when he registered for the draft. He was described by *The Freeborn County Standard* as a "Former Albert Lea Boy." He died in a plane crash on August 1st, 1918. In a cruel twist of fate, on August 26th, nearly four weeks after his death but before his death was known, The *Freeborn County Standard* printed a long letter from Prentice to his family. Originally published in the *Fairmont Sentinel,* and dated July 20, his letter went into detail about his flying experiences and the French countryside. When he was killed, Prentice was the observation officer on a bombing flight over enemy territory. Initial reports indicated Prentice and the pilot may have descended safely and been taken prisoner. The men were listed as missing in action for more than two months, an agonizing period for their families. *The Freeborn County Standard*'s report on August 26th, 1918 stated that Mrs. Prentice, who lived in Albert Lea and bravely held out hope for weeks, "was nearly prostrated by the shock of the news."

Another airman, Austin native Charles Seymour Johnson was killed in action over the battlefields of Flanders August 13th, 1918. In June of 1917, Johnson enlisted in the Royal Flying Corps; he was trained in Canada, and flew for the Royal Air Force (RAF). At first, he was a part of the 99th Squadron, RAF, based at Salisbury Plain, England. He served in France as part of the 206th squadron RAF. When his squadron of six was attacked by 30 German planes, their "only recourse was to flee." Seeing one of the planes in trouble, Johnson turned back to assist. "The two machines held their own in a terrific struggle for several moments but shortly both of them were seen to fall and we knew that blue eyed Charlie, the best loved soldier in the British flying service had gone to his death."[79]

Throughout the summer of 1918, the German army was continually pushed east. The cost in blood was high, but the addition of American troops was making a crucial difference for the western allies as they drove the enemy out of France.

The German high command, considering their bleak situation, was forced to consider the possibility of losing the war. For Erich Ludendorff, commanding general on the Western Front, August 18th, 1918, was "the black day of the German army."[80] Heavy fighting with the British near the town of Amiens finally convinced General Ludendorff that Germany could not prevail. His soldiers were exhausted and demoralized, food was short, and battlefield losses were impossible to replace. The Kaiser was given the grim news, and Ludendorff offered his resignation, but Kaiser Wilhelm II, and General von Hindenburg refused to accept i[illegible]erate, Germany resorted to conscripting young boys and old men. The "Kaiser's Battle" was over. From that day on the Germans fought defensively, no doubt hoping they could hold on long enough to achieve more favorable terms in some sort of negotiated peace. Still, for the AEF, including many soldiers from southern Minnesota, the hardest fighting and heaviest losses were yet to come. Most of those losses came in late 1918 as the Allies pushed the Central Powers east after their gains in the "Kaiser's Battle." Many American casualties occurred only days or hours before the war's end. The war continued until 11 a.m. on November 11th, 1918.

---

79. Nicholsen, Mower County in the World War, 13.

80. John Toland, *No Man's Land*, (New York, Konecky and Konecky, 1980), 373.

One local Minnesotan, Sergeant Palmer O. Narveson, the rural Albert Lea farmer who was denied a deferment to stay home and help on his father's farm, had a unique story. Narveson arrived in France on May 11th, 1918, just five months before the war ended. During that time, he was plunged into the thick of things and had to leave the trenches and go "over the top" eight times in one month. On September 29th, "He was the means of breaking up two machine gun nests in the face of great odds."[81] He was decorated for exceptional bravery by both the French and United States governments for his part in an operation near Bellicourt France.

Armistice Day, 1919, was special for Narveson who was re-established as a civilian by then. According to the November 17th edition of The *Freeborn County Standard,* General L. Collardet, French Military Attache and Special Representative of Marshall Foch, the Commander of the French army, journeyed from Washington D.C. to Minneapolis where he pinned the *Croix de Guerre,* a French medal for heroism, on Narveson's chest. The ceremony was described by the *Standard* as "elaborate and imposing." For Sergeant Narveson, Company H, 119th infantry, there was another honor, this one from the U.S. On July 24th, 1919, General Pershing announced that Narveson was to be awarded the *Distinguished Service Cross,* the second highest military award that can be given to a member of the U.S. Army. It is awarded for extreme gallantry in combat. *The Freeborn County Standard* reported the full text of the citation:

> For extraordinary heroism in action near Bellicourt France, September 29, 1918. When he and two soldiers, separated from the rest of the company, were fired upon from three directions, he attacked and demolished a machine gun nest by himself and

81. Wood, *In the World War: Freeborn County.*

The Distinguished Service Cross
and the Croix de Guerre.
Palmer Narveson was awarded both medals.

> then reduced a second hostile position. Though wounded and slightly gassed, he refused to be evacuated and continued the advance.

Another Freeborn County hero emerged during the summer of 1918. His name was Aage W. Swenson. Swenson, a truck driver, enlisted when he was nineteen. He had a way with words, and he made his daring deed seem almost as heroic as those of Sergeant Alvin York, the Tennessee soldier and Medal of Honor recipient who killed 25 and captured 132 Germans. His exploits, described in a letter to his sister, were published in the August 26th, 1918 edition of the *Freeborn County Standard*. Swenson, a private in Company F, 38th infantry regiment AEF, wrote of the daring escapade:

> I heard one afternoon of 40 wounded American soldiers that had been captured by the huns in a town quite a ways from where I was. No one thought it possible to rescue them from the Germans that were guarding them. I reasoned that they had had nothing to eat for 24 hours and would not put up much of a fight. I got some more boys to go with me. We took my truck and drove over. Once we arrived there we hid behind an old stone wall. We commenced to fire at the huns immediately. Some of them ran away. We finally encircled the rest and held them up while some of the others got the wounded on the truck. We then told the remaining Germans to beat it while the beating was good which they did. I got all of the 40 soldiers to a hospital. For this act the officers promoted me to Sergeant. Our regiment has just won the French "Croix de Guerre" so we will have a big time when it is fastened to our flag. And don't worry about us as we will all soon be home to stay.

The AEF fought in two major battles during the closing weeks of the war, at Blanc-Mont and the Meuse-Argonne. Today, the fight at Blanc-Mont Ridge is often overlooked, but in October of 1918, it took the U.S. Marines 24 days of hard fighting to dislodge the German army from heavily fortified positions atop the ridge. Blanc-Mont, east of Reims, and west of the Argonne Forest, was an important strategic prize. From the crest of the ridge, the rolling hills of the Champagne region in northeastern France unfold. A visitor to the summit can easily grasp its importance.

In October 1918, the AEF, both army and marines, paid in

blood to control the Ridge when it was once again called upon to relieve exhausted French forces. Led by Major General John A. Lejeune, United States Marine Corps (USMC), the battle was mainly a Marine operation, although elements of the U.S. army fought there as well. Nearly 8,000 Americans, both army and marines, were killed or wounded.

A strategic vista. The view from the summit of Blanc-Mont in 2015. Myron Herried was wounded here on October 6th, 1918.
Photo courtesy of Karen Herreid.

Myron Herreid, the marine aboard the troopship *Von Steuben* when it collided with *Agamemnon,* was wounded by shellfire at Blanc-Mont. His jaw was shattered by shrapnel on October 6th, 1918. He was awarded a Silver Star for his heroic actions on the Ridge.

Thomas Virgil William Meighen, a 25-year-old LeRoy area farmer, was also wounded at Blanc-Mont on October 4th, 1918. He died of his wounds October 19th, 1918, in a Red Cross hospital in Paris. "He was assisting in the comfort of a wounded comrade at the time he fell victim to a shell."[82] Meighen had close family connections in Fillmore, Mower, and Freeborn Counties. Freeborn and Mower County histories both list Meighen among the fallen from their respective counties.

The final great battle of the war for America was at the Meuse-Argonne. It was named for the Argonne Forest and the Meuse River, and was fought on a huge battlefield, the front 24 miles long. Located in Eastern France near the borders of both Belgium and Luxembourg, the Meuse-Argonne was, in a sense, the climax of the war for the AEF. Today, the Argonne Forest looks peaceful enough from a distance. A closer look reveals long, abandoned trenches and shell-churned earth that still bears witness to the fighting that marked Imperial Germany's end in November of 1918.

The Meuse-Argonne offensive was the American part of the final allied offensive which was fought all along the western front. French personnel were present, but it was mainly an American operation. Most troops were, for the first time, under overall American command. With so many men involved along a broad front, it was initially an unwieldy, disorganized mess. Accounts of the battle suggest that Pershing was not an effective commander. Apparently, he was unwilling to delegate responsibility to his subordinates until High Command in Washington D.C. intervened. Eventually, organization improved but was never especially efficient with such masses of men and material.[83]

The Meuse-Argonne remains the largest military engagement

82. Nicholsen, *Mower County in the World War*, 15.

83. Toland, *No Man's Land*, 429, 481.

and victory in U.S. history. About 1.2 million Americans were involved. American forces suffered 75,000 casualties, 26,000 of them killed and the rest injured. Forty percent of all Americans killed in action during World War One were killed at the Meuse-Argonne in the final two months of the war.

The battle began on September 26th, 1918. The AEF's initial objective was to seize a major rail junction in the area, one the German army needed for resupply. Since the junction was a strategic prize, the German army fought fiercely to hold it. The battle lasted until the Armistice on November 11th, 1918.

Artillery captain Harry Truman was also at the Meuse-Argonne together with George C. Marshall. Colonel Marshall was responsible for the logistics. Moving half a million American troops and their equipment into place over narrow French roads was a formidable challenge, but Marshall's planning made it possible. George Patton fought his first tank battle at the Meuse-Argonne, and Douglass MacArthur, already a General, was decorated nine times for his leadership and bravery. As fate would have it, those four men helped lead America to victory in another "Great War" a generation later. Regarding the horrors of Meuse-Argonne, Walter Hartman wrote:

> September--29--We caught up with the company just before they went on the firing line. We went up to the front lines and formed our own scrimmage line and all lie [sic] down and wait for orders to go over the top. We are in the direct fire of machine gunners and snipers and believe me we sure hug the ground. Our artillery puts up a barrage at 4:30 PM and we go over the top. And believe me you sure think of all the good and bad things you ever done.

> But that dont [sic] stop us, machine gun bullets, HE, [sic] and shrapnel bursting all around us. How anyone could go through such a hell is a mystery to me. We gained our objective and held in the face of the main flank fire, in this attack we had 4 killed and 35 wounded. It's a wonder we're not all dead. I had several narrow escapes. The good Lord sure was with me. [84]

Many other southern Minnesota soldiers were there too, and some of them died. Joseph Dyrdal of Oakland was killed October 6. Clarence Butler, was killed October 9th, 1918, fighting in the Verdun sector. He was a Freeborn County native, from Newry township. Gilbert Frondal, also from Oakland, was killed October 14. Dyrdal was thought to be part of the "Lost Battalion" in the Argonne Forest. The battalion, part of the AEF's 77th division, was isolated and surrounded by German forces in the Argonne Forest for nearly a week, suffering heavy losses before being rescued. Today, the "Lost Battalion" is the stuff of legend, the subject of books, articles, and at least one movie (a 2001 made-for-TV epic starring Ricky Schroder). Louis Tvette from Emmons was killed while fighting hand to hand. Other Freeborn County soldiers, including Simon Stenhood, Frank Suren, Daniel Schue, William Pegum, Albert Ohm, Ira Nelson, Freemond Madson, Hans Lundberg, Andrew Jenson, and Daniel Haynes were all killed in the Argonne: fourteen young men from Freeborn County, killed in a single battle, and of course, others were wounded. It was a huge toll for a county with less than 25,000 total population.[85]

The experience was much the same in other counties. In Mow-

84. Hartmann, Diary, 28.

85. Wood, *In the World War: Freeborn County.*

er County, the losses were great. Austin resident John Doyle was killed at the Meuse-Argonne, so too was former Hormel employee John Frederich. Frederich was recommended for the Distinguished Service Cross for his gallant service (see photo page 99). Nels Finkelson of Adams and LeRoy native Earl Frisbee both died at the Argonne. So did Floyd Griffin, Nay Harris, Walter Jacobson, Albert Nagle, Irwin Pettit, Leonard Pickett, Iver Thompson, Anton Torgerson, George Wilson, Peter Schmitt, and Glen Tatham.[86]

Not all soldiers served on the frontline. Many served in rear areas doing the hard work of supplying the fighting men with everything they needed to carry on. Some served in clerical roles, while others, like Oscar Holtz of Mower County, were cooks. Asa Hovey of Dexter was an aircraft mechanic.[87] Others did the essential work of caring for the wounded.

The United States provided about one million horses to its allies during the war. Government agents actively looked for horses to buy throughout southern Minnesota. The AEF itself had about 200,000 horses shipped to France. Providing transport, feed, tack, and other necessary supplies for them was a tremendous logistical challenge that required many men. Besides the enormous effort required to care for them, using horses had another drawback. When they were killed during the summer heat, the stench of decaying horseflesh was unbearable.

It has been said that "an army runs on its stomach," and one Mower County soldier distinguished himself in the important area of food supply. Feeding the AEF in France was a huge logistical challenge, one that Jay Hormel of Austin understood. Hormel, inducted on September 5th, 1917, was the first Minnesotan to report to Camp Dodge. Initially assigned to an infantry regiment, he was

86. Nicholsen, *Mower County in the World War*, 7-19.

87. Nicholson, *Mower County*, 95.

soon transferred to the Quartermaster Corps where his expertise in the meat industry was invaluable. Promotions followed rapidly for Hormel. On August 5th, 1918, he was promoted to first lieutenant. Soon after he received the promotion, he recommended that beef bound for France be deboned before shipment. He even demonstrated how it should be done. Hormel's idea was accepted, and he was credited with saving a significant amount of money in shipping costs.[88] On October 23rd, 1918, the *Mower County Transcript-Republican* reported that lieutenant Hormel was home, and that he had "been for some time looking after meat supplies for the Allied countries."

After Meuse-Argonne, Germany and her allies were finished. Bulgaria had capitulated in September 1918. The Ottoman Empire signed an armistice October 30. Austria-Hungary followed suit on November 3rd, 1918, when officials signed *The Armistice of Villa Giusti*. German High Command had long known victory was unattainable, and cynicism reigned. General Ludendorff, concerned with his role in history, wanted the Kaiser and Chancellor to request an armistice before the German army suffered a catastrophic defeat. He was looking for scapegoats, and he even suggested that the Kaiser appoint liberal and socialist ministers to end the war. They would bear the burden of defeat, not the Kaiser, Ludendorff, and the army's General Staff. [89]

Germany got its armistice, although not on the terms it wanted, and it was negotiated by new ministers. It went into effect at 11:00 a.m. on November 11th, 1918. Fighting continued, and soldiers died until literally the last minute even though it was known

88. Richard Dougherty, *In Quest of Quality: Hormel's First 75 Years*, (Austin Minnesota, George A. Hormel and Company, 1966), 133.

89. Holger H. Herwig, *The First World War: Germany and Austria-Hungary 1914-1918 2nd Edition*, (London, Bloomsbury, 2014), 410.

The Blooming Prairie Times.

VOLUME XXVII BLOOMING PRAIRIE, STEELE COUNTY, MINNESOTA, THURSDAY, NOVEMBER 14, 1918 NUMBER 24

Democracy Has Won
Victory-Peace-Safety

OUR FLAG

GERMAN ENVOYS ACCEPT ALLIED TERMS OF TRUCE

BURNQUIST AND NELSON CARRY COUNTY BY BIG PLURALITIES

Ditlevson, Kenyon and Pratt Defeat Opponents

Dr. B. Melby Elected Coroner

Official Steele County Election Returns

PEACE NEWS COME TRUE

BLOOMING PRAIRIE FALLS IN LINE AND HAS DOUBLE PEACE JUBILEE.

WAR WORK DRIVE A SUCCESS HERE

PROMPT PAYMENT OF REQUIRED ALLOTMENT THE RULE.

Two More Soldier Boys Pass Away

LESTER CREEGAN PASSES AWAY AT MILITARY CAMP AND EARTHLY CAREER OF HENRY HOLSTENSON ENDS IN FRANCE.

Lester Creegan.
The relatives and friends of

Henry B. Holstenson.
The sad news that Henry B.

Joy and sorrow on the front page.
The war was over, but influenza still claimed
the lives of soldiers and residents.
The Blooming Prairie Times,
November 14th, 1918.

6

INFLUENZA

"A large number of the soldier boys in training camp are victims of the now prevalent disease, Spanish influenza, says the Ellendale Eagle."
–*The People's Press,* October 11th, 1918

HANSEN, GEORGE PAUL
"Died of influenza and pneumonia,
Camp Hancock, October 4th, 1918"[91]

"Because of the Spanish influenza in several of the rural communities, some of the rural schools have been closed indefinitely."
–*Freeborn County Standard,* October 17th, 1918

"The big auction sale of Aberdeen Angus cattle which was scheduled to take place next Tuesday, October 29, at Otranto, has been postponed on account of the epidemic quarantine until a later date."
–*Mower County Transcript,* October 23rd, 1918

91. Nicholsen, *Mower County in the World War,* 11

"A grownup daughter of Nels Lostegaard, who lives near Red Oak Grove Church, died Tuesday night of pneumonia after an illness of about a week."
—*The People's Press,* November 15th, 1918

Bad news was everywhere in 1918. The war dominated the headlines, with heavy fighting at the Meuse-Argonne. Most editions carried the names of local casualties. On October 12th, a forest fire moved through the Cloquet-Moose Lake area in northern Minnesota; over 450 people were killed, and property damage ran in the millions of dollars. To make matters worse, influenza, by then a global pandemic, swept through every community, sickening, and sometimes killing residents.

Although often referred to as "Spanish influenza," there is no universal agreement as to the source of the virus. Most countries censored news reports during the war. Stories detrimental to the war effort were suppressed, including stories about the flu and its effects. Spain was neutral and did not impose such restrictions on its reporters. So, when Spanish king Alfonso was stricken with influenza, the news was widely disseminated. Soon, people were associating the disease with Spain, and the term "Spanish Influenza" came into widespread use even though health officials did not believe it was of Spanish origin.

Before it was over, the virus infected about 500 million people worldwide. Mortality estimates vary widely, from 17 to 50 million or more. While the actual number is unknown, it was devastating—one of the worst pandemics in recorded history.

The first case in the United States appeared among the soldiers at Fort Riley Kansas in January of 1918. By spring, the flu had spread to thousands of troops. As soldiers were shipped overseas, they brought the disease with them.

> Influenza sailed with American troops across the Atlantic and when it exploded in late August and September in Europe and the United States, medical officers found themselves on the front lines of an epidemic worse than any of them had ever seen or imagined. Many were among the most knowledgeable and skilled physicians in the country and had just recently entered military service. They did their best to save those stricken by influenza, but could do little more than provide palliative care of warmth, rest, and a gentle diet, and hope that their patients did not develop pneumonia.[92]

From September to November 1918, influenza affected 20% to 40% of all U.S. Army and Navy personnel, home and abroad. The disease rendered hundreds of thousands of military personnel ineffective. Resources, especially during the Meuse-Argonne campaign, were diverted from fighting the war to caring for the sick and dead.[93]

Influenza or complications arising from it accounted for over half of all the deaths of American servicemen during the war. Many of the deaths occurred in training camps which were quarantined. Camp Dodge, where many Minnesotans trained, had one of the worst training camp illness records with 13,700 hospitalizations and 700 deaths.[94]

Of the 64 Mower County servicemen who died during the war, 36 died of disease and 27 of those were in stateside camps at the

92. Carol R. Byerly, "The U.S. Military and the Influenza Pandemic of 1918-1919," *Public Health Reports* 125, Supplement 23 (2010): 82-91.
93. Byerly, *U.S. Military and Influenza.*
94. Ibid.

time.[95] The percentages are similar in Freeborn and Steele Counties. Not every death from disease was caused by the flu, but most were.

Sometimes influenza was quick as well as deadly. Peter Mullenbach, an Adams area farmer, did not even make it to a training camp. He entered service October 24th, 1918, and died enroute to Camp Cody.[96]

In one case, the January 23rd, 1919, issue of the *Blooming Prairie Times* reported that Edwin Jolson arrived home from Camp Penyman, Virginia after being honorably discharged. "He is hale and hearty," the article concluded. In an adjacent column, the Times reported on the death of Edwin's brother Hans, who was not called up—a victim of pneumonia and influenza. Edwin learned of his

95. Nicholsen, *Mower County*, 5.

96. Ibid., 15.

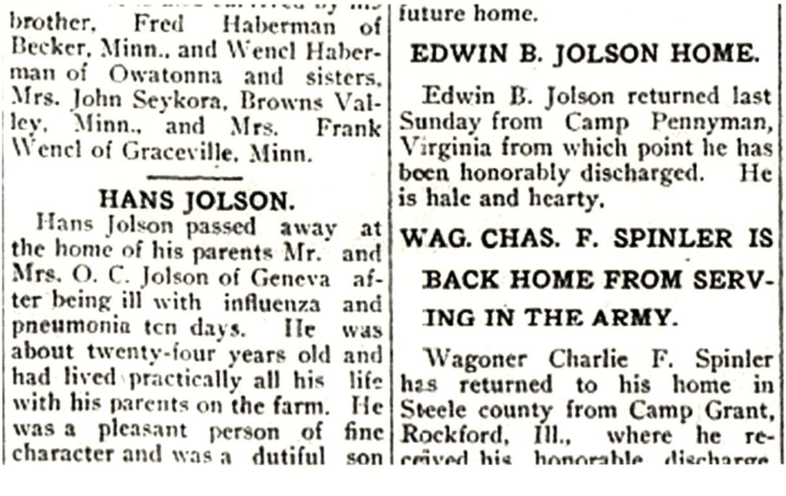

brother, Fred Haberman of Becker, Minn., and Wencl Haberman of Owatonna and sisters, Mrs. John Seykora, Browns Valley, Minn., and Mrs. Frank Wencl of Graceville, Minn.

HANS JOLSON.

Hans Jolson passed away at the home of his parents Mr. and Mrs. O. C. Jolson of Geneva after being ill with influenza and pneumonia ten days. He was about twenty-four years old and had lived practically all his life with his parents on the farm. He was a pleasant person of fine character and was a dutiful son

future home.

EDWIN B. JOLSON HOME.

Edwin B. Jolson returned last Sunday from Camp Pennyman, Virginia from which point he has been honorably discharged. He is hale and hearty.

WAG. CHAS. F. SPINLER IS BACK HOME FROM SERVING IN THE ARMY.

Wagoner Charlie F. Spinler has returned to his home in Steele county from Camp Grant, Rockford, Ill., where he re-

Jolson Brothers.

Blooming Prairie Times, January 23rd, 1919.

brother's death when he was met at the train depot by his family.

In a cruel twist, the disease was particularly deadly to young people in the prime of their lives. Millions of people in their 20s and early 30s died worldwide. Fatality rates were highest in the healthiest populations. Scientists were baffled. Other than bedrest, doctors did not have any effective treatment options. It was awful to witness a robust young person afflicted with fever, hemorrhaging with pneumonia, and drowning as their lungs filled with fluid.

Not only was the disease deadly, efforts to control it caused dissent. Debate raged over whether schools and businesses should be closed and for how long. In Austin, citizens were divided. School officials and the Board of Health felt that students were better off in school where they could be supervised by the school nurse. Not everyone agreed. The Austin City Council passed a resolution prohibiting public gatherings and "among which was the closing of schools." On October 23rd, 1918, the *Mower County Transcript-Republican* described it this way:

> The Board of Health closed all but the schools and with the advice of the State Board of Health the schools still remain in session. This has developed a merry war which we hope will be settled for the best interests of the public in general. In many instances schools have been closed in other towns.

In Austin, passions ran high and led to a fistfight on main street between Mayor George Hirsh and local Health Director, Dr. C.F. Lewis. The incident was widely reported, even statewide in the *Minneapolis Tribune*. On October 23rd, it made the front page of the *Austin Weekly Herald*: "The clash between mayor Hirsch and Dr. C. F. Lewis, chairman of the city Board of Health reached a climax today when

Two Blooming Prairie Soldiers Die in Georgia

INFLUENZA HAS CLAIMED DUGAN A VICTIM.

Blooming Prairie Boy Succumbs Following Attack of Pneumonia.

His Death Occurred at Camp Hancock.

KUBICEK VICTIM OF PNEUMONIA.

Joseph Kubicek, Former Blooming Prairie Boy, Succumgs to Pneumonia at Camp Hancock, Augusta, Georgia.

Many soldiers died of influenza in the training camps.
Blooming Prairie Times, January 23rd, 1919.

doctor Lewis drew off and hit the mayor a blow on the side of the face and got a comeback blow on the arm from the mayor."

Hirsch and Lewis were both dedicated public servants, tireless in service to their community. Perhaps the stress of dealing with the war and the pandemic lead to the main-street fisticuffs.

"School closed Monday evening for the remainder of the week on account of the attendance being so small on account of the influenza scare," was the notice that appeared in the October 24th, issue of the *Freeborn County Standard*. It concerned the Geneva school. By October of 1918, the flu was everywhere, and it was deadly. Many schools, town and country alike, closed, often not reopening until after the holidays.

The flu was still active in 1919, but in a less virulent form than in 1918. As servicemen were sent home, and camps depopulated, the virus had less fuel to work with. The twin scourges of war and influenza were over.

7

BUY BONDS

"FREEBORN COUNTY PEOPLE STIRRED BY GREAT LIBERTY LOAN DEMONSTRATION"
–*Freeborn County Standard,* April 8th, 1918

War is expensive in terms of lives and property lost or ruined, but also in money—huge sums of money. With the onset of war, America's question quickly became, "How do we pay for it?"

The process of financing the war through the sale of Liberty Bonds is a good example of people working together in a time of crisis. Like other aspects of life during the war, it showed the high level of intolerance directed toward those few who chose not to participate. When Congress authorized the bonds, they had to be sold. There was widespread enthusiasm for the idea and community involvement in its execution. Many people volunteered to organize the bond drives, soliciting in their neighborhoods and investing as much as they could.

In the hyper-patriotic atmosphere of 1917 and 1918, people had little tolerance for those reluctant to participate. Everyone who was financially able was expected to purchase bonds and support the war effort. Those who refused to purchase their "fair share" of the Liberty Bonds were singled out. Their patriotism was ques-

"Hello! This is liberty speaking - billions of dollars are needed and needed now."
Z.P. Nikolaki, 1918. Wikimedia Commons.

tioned. Sometimes they were called "slackers," and failure to purchase could mean serious social and/or economic repercussions. Over the course of the war, the methods used to bring people in line became more and more coercive. The term "Liberty Loans" is misleading. Minnesotans were persecuted for exercising their "liberty" to not participate in the bond drives.

The American war effort cost billions. Federal spending rose exponentially in the war years from $1.3 billion in 1916 to $15.6 billion in 1918. An additional $12.4 billion was spent in 1919. In all, the total cost of the war for the U.S. was about $33 billion (approximately 577 billion in current U.S. dollars). Added to that was the complicated issue of war loans to other nations. American banks and the government loaned additional billions primarily to Britain and France. How and where could the United States, a nation with a relatively small military establishment, raise the money necessary for such a vast expansion of its fighting capabilities? Simply put, there were three ways to do it: 1) raise taxes, 2) use the Federal Reserve to create money, or 3) borrow from the public.

TAX

For taxation, Congress created the War Revenue Act. Essentially, the Act increased taxes on income, increased excise taxes, created a new luxury tax and an excess profit tax. The new tax revenue was important, but in raising just $7.3 billion, it did not come close to matching the need for additional funds.

CREATE

The Federal Reserve did create money in various ways. For example, purchasers of large denomination bonds, of at least $1,000 were encouraged to "borrow to buy." They could borrow the money from their bank, purchase the bond, and the Federal Reserve would then lend that amount back to the bank at a low rate of interest. However, with the United States on the gold standard and with recent memories of the inflationary Civil War-era Green Backs, economists were generally uneasy with the option.

BORROW

That meant the third leg of the stool, borrowing from the public, was essential in filling the gap between federal income and expenses. Therefore, beginning in April 1917, and continuing for the duration of the war, Congress authorized the issue of Liberty Bonds four times. The fifth and final issue, called the "Victory Bond," was floated in early 1919. A War Savings Stamp program for smaller investors was also put in place. In total, the government borrowed about $24 billion from the public: about 400 billion in 2020 dollars.

First, Congress passed the Emergency Loan Act authorizing the sale of what were generally known as "Liberty" bonds. The first tranche was issued on April 24th, 1917. It provided for the issuance of $5 billion in bonds at 3.25% interest. The legislation made the Federal Reserve Bank responsible for issuing the debt and handling the proceeds. The pattern was the same for all five loan drives. Each Federal Reserve district was given an allotment which was then divided among the states in its district. When the last drive was complete, Minnesota, a part of the ninth Federal Reserve District, had been allotted a total of $410,000,000. The state allotment was then divided up among the counties, then therewith subdivided among the individual county's cities, villages, and townships.

The size of the allotment was based on each county's "banking resources," or wealth based on bank deposits, not, as one might assume, on population. For example, Freeborn and Mower Counties had similar-sized populations during World War I, yet the Mower County allotment for liberty loans was always higher than its neighbor to the west. In the second liberty loan, Mower County even had a higher allotment than the more heavily populated Olmsted County.[97]

Treasury Secretary William McAdoo saw the need for more ef-

97. Nicholson, *Mower County*, 210.

fective means to market the bonds to the public, especially after the first loan was not particularly well received. As a result, the Federal Government through its recently created propaganda bureau, the Committee on Public Information (CPI), created nationwide campaigns to sell them. There were a wide variety of marketing strategies employed. Some featured celebrities. Charlie Chaplin made a movie, "The Bond," extolling the virtues of Liberty Bonds. Propaganda posters were employed, and a speaker's bureau was established. In some parts of the country, air shows featuring aerobatics by pilots in the famous Curtiss "Jenny" biplanes were used as sales tools.

Recent immigrants, eager to prove their support for the war, found that "buying bonds, singing the national anthem in public, and displaying the American flag became important symbols of national loyalty."[98] McAdoo later justified the use of propaganda, pointing out that "any great war must necessarily be a popular movement. It is a kind of crusade . . . it sweeps along on a popular stream of romanticism." [99]

The bond drives were about much more than just raising money. Americanizing recent immigrants and generally binding all Americans together for a great cause were important too. The process had both positive and negative aspects. In southern Minnesota, the Steele County experience is a good example.

Former State Senator and a chairman of the second loan drive campaign in Steele County, Thomas Cashman, was a pioneer of sorts in developing methods to coerce people into buying. In Steele County, failure to purchase meant being recorded on "Blue Cards." Cashman believed the cards to be "worth their weight in gold."

---

98. James J. Kimble, *Mobilizing the Home Front: War Bonds and Domestic Propaganda* (College Station: Texas A&M University Press, 2006), 4.

99. Ibid.

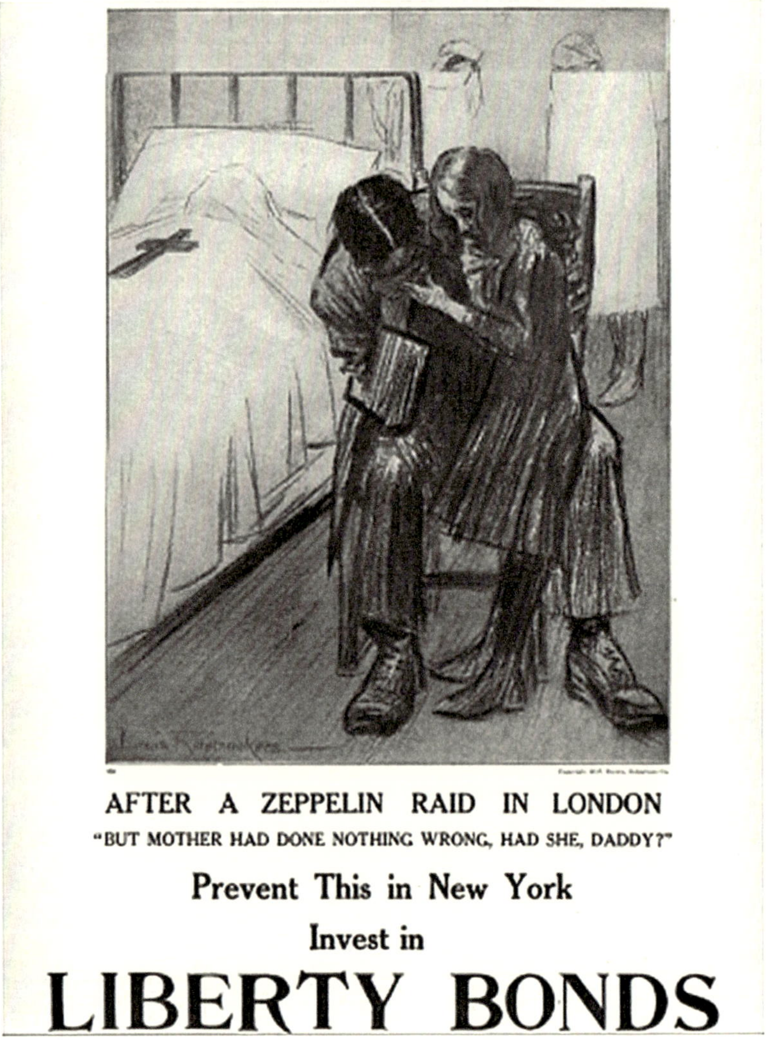

"After a Zeppelin Raid in London: "But Mother Had Done Nothing Wrong, Had She, Daddy?" Prevent this in New York: Invest in Liberty Bonds."
Louis Raemaekers, propaganda, 1917.
Rutgers University Library collection.

> When the average man finds that he is going to be reported to his government, giving in detail the amount of property he owns and his reasons for not subscribing, he usually calls up those who are carrying on the campaign and wants further information and then usually comes across . . .
>
> This Liberty Bond Campaign has done wonders towards making seditious people loyal in this county.[100]

Evidently, the "Blue Cards" captured people's attention. On Sunday October 21st, 1917, the *Owatonna Daily People's Press* reported:

> Blue Cards are disappearing from Steele County's files. The special committee working in the country yesterday returned with several subscriptions from persons who earlier in the campaign had turned in blue cards. Misunderstandings of the salient feature of the liberty loan seem to have been responsible for the bulk of the blue cards. Also, several persons whose names were on "blue cards" called at Liberty Loan headquarters and made subscriptions. Their "blue cards" were destroyed and the application for Liberty Bonds were accepted. They said they had not understood the government's plan until after conversations with the first committee and that since they had learned they were ready to back the government.

100. Carl H. Chrislock, *Watchdog of Loyalty: The Minnesota Public Safety Commission During World War I* (St. Paul: Minnesota Historical Society Press, 1991), 224.

Whether it was a "misunderstanding," patriotism, a good interest rate, or a combination of variables, the tactics worked. When the books were closed on the second drive, Steele County residents had purchased $460,000 in Liberty Bonds.

Bells and whistles, and one may assume a celebratory drink or two, marked the end of the successful bond campaign in Blooming Prairie. In its celebratory account of the drive, The *Blooming Prairie Times* headline on October 18th, 1917, gleefully proclaimed, " . . . Their [sic] Are No Slackers Here." The Times even published a list of purchasers, street by street. J. C. Brainard and B. Betlach each bought $500 in bonds. Albert Rye, Frank Ruzek, Olga Peterson Nelson, A.S. Srsen and many other Blooming Prairie residents invested from $50-$200. Banker and politician Sam Rask topped them all with a $1,000 bond investment. As a rule of thumb, one dollar in 1917 was equivalent to $17-$18 today, making the size of purchases remarkable, especially considering that only six months had passed since the first drive.

Blue cards were used in other counties too. Solicitors in Mower County carried two cards, white cards for buyers and the blue "slacker" cards for those who refused to buy. The blue cards featured a variety of intrusive, personal questions designed to stimulate buying. If non-buyers could not be convinced in any other way, a "Dynamiting Committee" was deployed. Their cry was "Get right with God and America." Their methods were not always gentle or even legal, and they did not always succeed in getting the money. The committee members nevertheless believed their efforts were worthwhile for future drives.[101]

Bonds were designed to be attractive to investors. Buying bonds did not require a financial sacrifice, and the interest rate was good; ranging from 3.25% to 4.75% depending on the issue. They

101. Nicholson, *Mower County*, 211.

Did You Buy A Liberty Bond? "Shall we be more tender with our dollars than we are with the blood of our sons?" W. G. McAdoo.

The Blooming Prairie Times.

VOLUME XXVI BLOOMING PRAIRIE, STEELE COUNTY, MINNESOTA, THURSDAY, OCTOBER 18, 1917. NUMBER 20

Over $31,000 Raised in Rousing Campaign Tuesday!

RED CROSS HARD AT WORK

Big Campaign for Members and Funds to be Launched in The Near Future.

ENTIRE DRAFT QUOTA MAY GO ON NEXT CALL

Present Moves Indicate That Group Entraining Plan Will Be Changed.

Farmers Organize Live Stock Company.

Organization Perfected At Meeting Held Saturday Evening, October 13th.

BOARD CALLS FOR 40 MORE DRAFT MEN

Fourth Contingent Will Be Examined October 18—List To Be Posted Today.

Liberty Bond Sales in Blooming Prairie and Vicinity Indicate That Their Are No Slackers Here.

Jubilation in Blooming Prairie with the results of the Second Liberty Bond Drive. Note the plea from Treasury Secretary W.G. McAdoo in the upper right corner.
Blooming Prairie Times, October 18th, 1917.

were convertible, meaning early issue bonds bearing an interest rate lower than later issues could be converted to the higher rate. Interest was exempt from certain types of taxes depending on the bond issue. That feature was offered to make the bonds attractive to a broad range of investors. At a time of stock market uncertainty, and bank and postal savings rates of 2-3%, they were a secure, attractive investment. For those lacking cash, banks were willing and eager to make loans for their purchase.[102]

An elaborate system was established to sell the bonds locally. At the county level, the overall responsibility was in the hands of community bankers. In southern Minnesota, bankers met soon after Congress authorized the sale and organized the loan campaign. The number of people involved in the local campaigns was remarkable.

102. Ibid., 215.

The campaign in Mower County began with the city of Austin. Bankers including three members of the Banfield family, W. W. Walker, and P. D. Beaulieu organized the first Liberty Loan campaign. The Austin Businessman's Association and the Austin Commercial Club were called upon to organize committees to "push the sale of Liberty Loan bonds."[103] A committee of four men, who were involved with the bankers in the canvassing process, was established in each of the city's three wards. Those men in turn recruited volunteers within their respective neighborhoods to do the actual soliciting. Prominent bankers and merchants in the city led the committees.

Leading citizens with names that many current Austin residents would still recognize, such as Crane, Hormel, Skinner, Scoville, Alderson, and others, were featured prominently in all five loan campaigns. In the city of Austin alone, 40 to 60 men per ward were active in the first campaign, a total of more than 150. The Hormel Packing company made it easy for its employees to contribute with a payroll deduction scheme.[104]

The situation in rural Mower County was much the same. Community bankers across the county recruited solicitors for each village and township. Responsibility in townships was divided down to individual sections. The entire county was covered from LeRoy to Lansing and Lyle to Racine. Eventually, the formula for rural areas became extremely detailed. For example, a November 6th, 1918, notice in the *Mower County Transcript* Republican instructed citizens of Udolpho Township to appear at the usual voting place and take their allotment. The allotment was defined as net worth times 0.0014.

The first loan campaign closed on June 15th, 1917, less than a month after the first countywide organizational meeting was held

103. Ibid., 206.

104. Ibid., 206.

in Austin. The Mower County allotment was $350,000. At the end of the campaign, Mower County subscriptions totaled $311,000. Given the limited time and "newness" of the proposition, the campaign was judged a success.

In Freeborn County, residents subscribed about $250,000 in the first campaign. Sixty percent of the total came from Albert Lea. The organizational structure was much the same as in Mower County. County bankers took charge, and men perhaps best described as "City Fathers" took leadership positions. Businessman Theodore Speltz was appointed overall chairman of the drive in the city of Albert Lea. All the villages and townships, as well as the city of Albert Lea, were covered. Women were prominent in the Freeborn County Drive. In the city of Albert Lea, a women's committee was established to solicit subscriptions specifically from women. The committee consisted of Miss Clara Peterson, Mrs. Jurene Haugdahl, and Miss Anna Frydenlund. "They did splendid work in interesting the women to buy bonds."[105]

Citizens were expected to buy their fair share of bonds. Naturally, that raised the question of what was "fair," and methods first adopted in drives two and three were improved and used in the fourth campaign. Steele County's improved, third drive was so effective that it was published by the Ninth Federal Reserve District in their newsletter *Liberty Bell*. Steele County was allotted $520,000 for the third loan, and raised $675,000; a great success.[106] This is how they did it:

> With us, preparation of the cards began February 1st and covered a period of exactly 4 weeks. Three persons devoted their entire time and to others at

105. Wood, *In the World War: Freeborn County.*

106. Holbrook and Appel, vol. 2 *Minnesota in the War with Germany*, 206.

> least two hours a day to the card index during this period. Every available source of information was drawn upon four names and their proper place things as to residents, real estate owned, personal property and indebtedness. During March, rating committees with a personnel [sic] beyond reproach met every weekday evening for over three weeks augmenting the information already obtained so that a conservative net with worth figure could be placed upon each card. An allotment of bonds was made on 2% of net worth, so that persons worth less than $5000 were simply allotted $100 or $50 in bonds.[107]

A committee sifted through the financial data of every property-owning citizen of Steele County and arbitrarily decided how much each was worth and how much each should invest. The allotment per person was set at 2% of net worth. The report goes on to say that the percentage of people who responded to the notice was high. In some districts, everyone who was notified came in. The net proceeds were 15% more than the allotment. The report concluded:

> The whole campaign proved a revelation to everyone involved. We have not yet recovered from the mystery. I believe that the publicity and curiosity as to the individual share were contributing factors in bringing so many in and once inside nearly every man seemed to catch the spirit and did his duty.[108]

107. Holbrook and Appel, vol. 2 *Minnesota,* 205.

108. Ibid., 206.

The Mower County experience was similar. Ralph P. Crane, an Austin businessman, served as chairman of both the third and fourth loan campaigns. He used the allotment system, dividing the county's share among the city of Austin and Mower County villages and townships. With more than 500 trained volunteers, the campaign committee spent weeks pouring over records of real estate and personal property taxes paid and records of contributions to other fund drives, including the Red Cross and YMCA. Based on the data they collected, each precinct was expected to raise 1% of the total property value in the precinct plus $40 per capita.

This plan did not satisfy everyone. Loan headquarters on Main Street in Austin was the scene of several arguments about the arbitrary nature of the allotments. "Many interesting scenes were enacted with this room and the various traits of human nature were abundantly displayed."[109] In spite of the protests, the Mower County drive began April 15th, 1918 with a quota of $750,000. By noon the next day, the drive concluded with over $1 million in liberty loan purchases.

Bert Skinner served as County Chairman for drives three and four in Freeborn County. The Freeborn County allotment in the third drive was $625,000. Skinner used the same tactic as that of Mower County and divided the allotment amongst the city of Albert Lea and all Freeborn County villages and townships. Albert Lea, the villages, and townships exceeded their allotment. Moscow and Newry townships in north eastern Freeborn County both went over their goals by about 15%. The third Freeborn County campaign raised $775,000.

Freeborn County reported the amount pledged by railroad companies as a separate item. In the third loan drive, the railroad company subscription was $10,000 and $18,200 in the fourth. In both cases, about 1.5% of the county total.[110]

109. Nicholson, *Mower County*, 206.

110. Wood, *In the World War: Freeborn County*.

Of the five loans, tranche four at $6 billion in September 1918 was the largest. The Freeborn and Mower County allotments, both in excess of $1 million, were nearly double those of the third drive conducted in April. Lessons learned in earlier drives were employed and enhanced. New tactics, positive and negative, were adopted. Motivational speakers of all sorts appeared. Ministers, war veterans, and government officials spoke wherever there was an audience. "Four-minute men" appeared in theaters, drumming up bond sales as the reels of film were being changed. Propaganda posters were everywhere.

For the flag waving super patriots, the coercive methods were not enough. Slackers were to be found, harassed, and, if necessary, publicly shamed if they could not be coerced into buying. To exercise your right or "liberty" and refuse to buy was to risk public humiliation and worse. The dark side to the business of selling Liberty Bonds was part of all the campaigns, but it reached a climax in late summer 1918 during the fourth loan. Attitudes hardened as there was less interest in a patriotic appeal and more emphasis on coercion.

The State of Minnesota set the tone with Public Safety Commission Order Number 44. The order gave local officials a license to trample on the rights of citizens. Published on August 27th, 1918, it gave extraordinary powers to County commission directors. The idea was to prod people "suspected of not being forthcoming in disclosing their assets to local bond committees."

The order itself is astonishing:

> The County Director of each County in the State, hereinafter called the "agent" is appointed the agent of the Commission with his County until further action by for the following purposes, with the following orders:

> On being advised at any time in writing by the then acting chairman, having in charge the promoting or sale of any pending issues of liberty loan bonds, that it is desirable or necessary to make investigation as to the property and resources of any person, a resident of the county, to the end that the amount of his proper subscription to such bonds may be determined, the agent may require such person, and any witnesses, to appear before him for examination at any convenient place in such county, may adjourn the hearings from time to time and from place to place in said county, may administer oaths, may examine such persons under oath as to any information within their knowledge pertaining to said investigations, and require such persons to produce for inspection any writings or documents under their control pertinent to said investigations, using for all and any such purposes any and all instrumentalities and proceedings specified in Chapter 261, Laws 1917, or otherwise permitted by law.[111]

The order was deadly serious. Individuals who refused to purchase their allotment for whatever reason were hounded by local agents of the Safety Commission. Some were summoned and compelled to testify under oath about the extent of their financial resources.

A report in the October 11th, 1918, issue of *The People's Press*, a weekly Owatonna newspaper, exemplified just how far the Commission was willing to go to enforce universal participation in the

111. J.A.A. Burnquist et al. *Report of Minnesota Commission of Public Safety*, St. Paul, Louis P. Dow Co, 125-126.

bond drives. After failing to report to Liberty Loan headquarters during the fourth loan drive, L.C. Palas, a Meriden area farmer, was obliged to provide financial statements under oath to the Steele County Public Safety Commission. Following the hearing, the board decided that Mr. Palas' fair share was $800, twice what the loan committee had originally sought. According to the board, it was not a penalty, but purely what Mr. Palas owed the government in the support of the war. The board claimed it was "his war as much as any other citizen of the United States." The local commission imposed the bond purchase on Pallas in part because he had not purchased bonds in any of the first three Liberty Loan drives, nor had he contributed to the Red Cross. Palas signed the subscription.

Not every case was the same, as *The People's Press* reported. The Steele County safety Commission did accept some excuses. Y.F. Pfiefer of Bixby, Minnesota was given a pass on the fourth loan because he had purchased bonds in the first three drives and had contributed to the Red Cross. However, most people summoned did finally agree to subscribe. Albert O. Anderson of Aurora signed for $200. Mr. Woodall of Lemond argued about his valuation, but in the end agreed to purchase. Woodall's subscription was $350.

There was an interesting Steele County case involving the Blooming Prairie branch of the Commission. William W. Wanous of that community voluntarily came to the Owatonna Commission to make his pledge. For some reason, Wanous did not care to do business with the Blooming Prairie Commission. With a $14,000 net worth, he agreed with the Owatonna agents that an allotment of $500 was his "fair share," even after being assigned $350 in Blooming Prairie. Newspaper accounts are not clear as to why Wanous agreed to pay more in Owatonna than Blooming Prairie.

The front-page headline in the October 10, 1918, edition of The *Freeborn County Standard* screamed: "Court Hearing on Bond

Slackers." The truth is they were not really "Court Hearings." The meetings were held in the offices of the fourth Liberty Loan Committee. Freeborn County board members included C.A. Chapman, Martin Blacklin, and Attorneys H.A. Morgan, N.E. Peterson, and H.A. Spencer. Committee chairman Bert Skinner convened the Freeborn County sessions which were even attended by a representative of the State Safety Commission.

The proceedings were conducted under oath and were "very broad and searching in scope." Subpoenas were issued and reports indicate that a representative of the federal government was present at the hearings. In a startling statement, the *Standard's* October 10th account indicates that it was believed the federal government had representatives in Freeborn County looking into reports of concealed income and grain.

The Freeborn County proceedings cleared up several "misunderstandings." After a short hearing, most people agreed to their quota. Those who were inclined to argue could do so, but the commission had the final say. There were at least sixteen "defendants" called before the Commission. Henry Ferguson of Newry Township was the first to appear. He agreed to his quota, as did Alfred Beck, Mrs. N.C. Nelson, and William J. Horning. Lars Norgaard and George Herr had their quotas reduced. There were others who did not give in easily.

The most difficult Freeborn County case was that of Mrs. Catherine Weigand. She appeared before the Commission with a "belligerent attitude." During the contentious hearing, Mrs. Weigand argued that she should not have to subscribe because she had given two boys to the army: one son who was then in the service and one who would be called up soon. She was reminded by Commissioner Morgan that her family had been accused of pro-German sentiments and that the community still considered her family as such. Morgan went on to say that her family had been opposed to all the war moves, and therefore they were decidedly disloyal. Ultimately, Weigand agreed to her quota.

The Weigand assessment, based partly on assets in an estate she shared with her sons, was $1,800. Considering the fact that her son, Carlyle Tunell Weigand, was sent to France just days after the October 1918 hearing, it seems that the Commission went out of their way to criticize, and publicly humiliate her, even though she did finally agree to the very large quota.

Like Mower County, most people in Freeborn and Steele Counties subscribed to the bond program. Generally, however, "the threat of a hearing brought the slackers to a realization that the patriotic people of Mower County were in earnest."[112] An observation in the October 2nd, 1918 edition *Mower County Transcript-Republican* expressed the popular view of the loan drive this way: "We understand that $28,000 was drawn out of the Lansing State Bank Saturday for the fourth Liberty Loan. Everyone responded cheerfully to the fourth call."

In contrast with the perceived cheer, the Sheriff served two District court Subpoenas on two Mower County men. They appeared before the County Safety Commission to answer why they should not support their government in time of war. Commission chairman W.A. Nolan, a Grand Meadow resident, presided. Attorneys J.N. Nicolson and F.G. Sasse questioned the men. A full report of the proceedings was given to the newspapers; of note: "They were given a grilling." The next day one of the men went to Rose Creek, where no one would speak to him. Furthermore, no tradesmen would sell to him. "He then paid his allotment and was again a man among men."[113]

Theoretically at least, failure to purchase was not an indictable offense. However, the extra-legal bullying, harassment and public

112. Nicholsen, *Mower County*, 257.

113. Nicholsen, *Mower County*, 257.

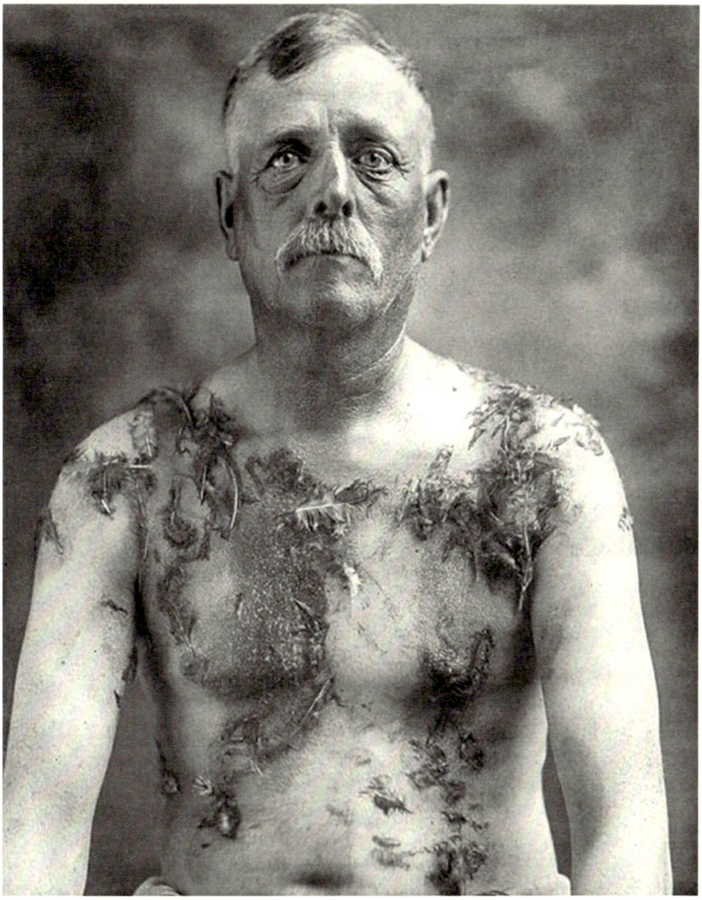

John Meints, tarred and feathered. The Luverne area farmer, a German immigrant, paid a heavy price for his "disloyalty."
Wikimedia Commons.

humiliation could be as painful as a jail sentence. Furthermore, Governor Burnquist had little sympathy for those who failed to purchase. A member of the Governor's staff bluntly told one Minnesota resident who complained that he had no money to purchase his allotment that while the law did not compel him to buy, it was the "duty of all patriotic citizens to do so." The response went on to say

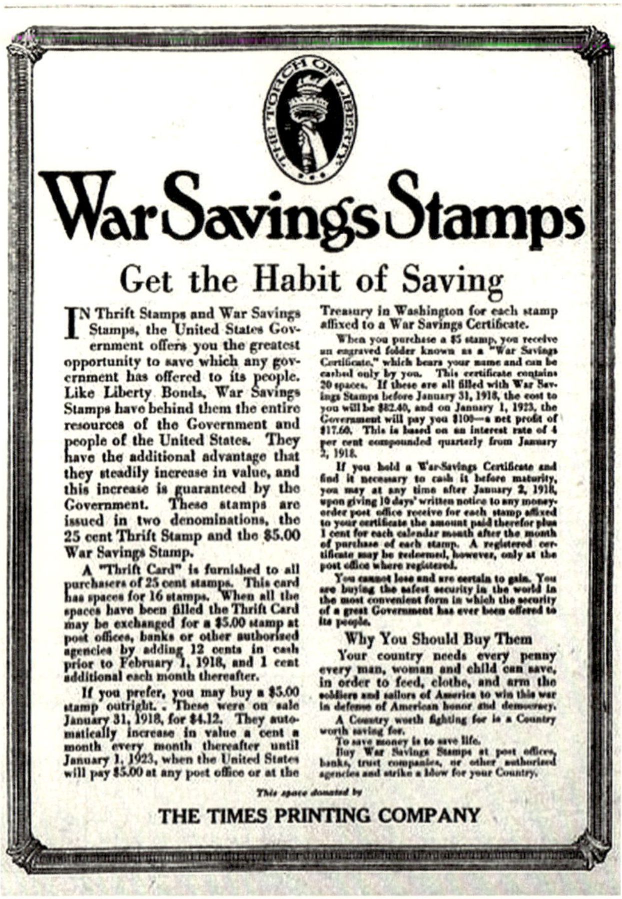

THE TORCH OF LIBERTY

War Savings Stamps

Get the Habit of Saving

IN Thrift Stamps and War Savings Stamps, the United States Government offers you the greatest opportunity to save which any government has offered to its people. Like Liberty Bonds, War Savings Stamps have behind them the entire resources of the Government and people of the United States. They have the additional advantage that they steadily increase in value, and this increase is guaranteed by the Government. These stamps are issued in two denominations, the 25 cent Thrift Stamp and the $5.00 War Savings Stamp.

A "Thrift Card" is furnished to all purchasers of 25 cent stamps. This card has spaces for 16 stamps. When all the spaces have been filled the Thrift Card may be exchanged for a $5.00 stamp at post offices, banks or other authorised agencies by adding 12 cents in cash prior to February 1, 1918, and 1 cent additional each month thereafter.

If you prefer, you may buy a $5.00 stamp outright. These were on sale January 31, 1918, for $4.12. They automatically increase in value a cent a month every month thereafter until January 1, 1923, when the United States will pay $5.00 at any post office or at the Treasury in Washington for each stamp affixed to a War Savings Certificate.

When you purchase a $5 stamp, you receive an engraved folder known as a "War Savings Certificate," which bears your name and can be cashed only by you. This certificate contains 20 spaces. If these are all filled with War Savings Stamps before January 31, 1918, the cost to you will be $82.40, and on January 1, 1923, the Government will pay you $100—a net profit of $17.60. This is based on an interest rate of 4 per cent compounded quarterly from January 2, 1918.

If you hold a War-Savings Certificate and find it necessary to cash it before maturity, you may at any time after January 2, 1918, upon giving 10 days' written notice to any money-order post office receive for each stamp affixed to your certificate the amount paid therefor plus 1 cent for each calendar month after the month of purchase of each stamp. A registered certificate may be redeemed, however, only at the post office where registered.

You cannot lose and are certain to gain. You are buying the safest security in the world in the most convenient form in which the security of a great Government has ever been offered to its people.

Why You Should Buy Them

Your country needs every penny every man, woman and child can save, in order to feed, clothe, and arm the soldiers and sailors of America to win this war in defense of American honor and democracy.

A Country worth fighting for is a Country worth saving for.

To save money is to save life.

Buy War Savings Stamps at post offices, banks, trust companies, or other authorized agencies and strike a blow for your Country.

This space donated by

THE TIMES PRINTING COMPANY

Savings Stamps for those who could not afford bonds.
Blooming Prairie Times, April 11th, 1918.

that jobs were plentiful, and everyone should be able to afford to buy at least a small bond.[114]

Extra-legal hearings, slacker cards, public humiliation, and even shunning were bad enough. Beyond some vague hints about methods "not always according to the law," there is no record of anyone in Freeborn, Steele, or Mower Counties being physically

114. Carl H. Chrislock, *Watchdog of Loyalty,* 288.

abused. That was not always the case in other places.

In August of 1918, John Meints, a German American farmer from Luverne (in southwestern Minnesota) was tarred, feathered, whipped, assaulted, and literally driven out of Minnesota for his supposed "disloyalty." Meints was told by his tormentors that he would be hanged if he returned to Minnesota. One of his alleged disloyal acts was not buying war bonds. After the war, Meints sued his attackers who were later acquitted. The jury refused to award him any damages. To add insult to injury, there was a celebration in Luverne when the verdict was returned.

Sometimes the failure to buy bonds was truly the result of a misunderstanding, and sometimes people had genuine, strongly held objections to purchasing. Whatever the reason, the price for exercising your rights and refusing to buy was high.

Today, it is hard to understand how people could so willingly turn upon their neighbors. It appears that the fear and hysteria of wartime in Minnesota caused many to lose their good judgment for a time. Some of the behavior may be explained by the fact that a century ago, a large percentage of Minnesotans were immigrants or the children of immigrants. Even those with family fighting in France were subject to abuse, as was the case with Mrs. Weigand. Civil liberties were trampled upon. The courts, which in normal times could be relied upon to protect the rights of citizens, instead reinforced the worst instincts of political leaders at the state and local level.

8

IT'S "BOOZY PRAIRIE"

"The little booze cursed village to the north
has decided by 32 to be the stench hole
of southern Minnesota."
–*Austin Weekly Herald,* March 13th, 1918

"When officer Sergeant stepped up to him at the depot Tony sacrificed the booze by breaking the bottles. The depot smelled like Blooming Prairie for some time afterwards."
–*Austin Weekly Herald,* date unknown

"Places of P.F. Coggins, W.R. Carrol and Geo. E. Thomas now guarded by men in uniform."
–*Blooming Prairie Times,* July 4th, 1918

"Great Booze Haul: State Safety Commission Agent Captures Bootlegger's Supply"
–*Blooming Prairie Times,* September 26th, 1918

In 1918, the editors of the *Herald* did not like what was happening in Blooming Prairie, and they were not afraid to show it. Their comments about the pleasant Steele County village emphasized just how toxic the liquor trade issue was in wartime Minnesota.

The story of the State of Minnesota versus the Blooming Prairie saloon owners in 1917 and 1918 is historically significant locally and statewide. It was a strange episode that pitted small, independent businessmen against the dictatorial powers of the Minnesota Commission of Public Safety. It was a continuation of a controversy that had been simmering in Minnesota politics for years.

Progressives, people who believed that society could be improved by legislating reforms like prohibition and women's suffrage, were politically powerful when the war broke out. In 1914, the Anti-saloon League and its allies, largely rural interests, won a working majority in both houses of the Minnesota Legislature. They argued that since all county residents were forced to pay the public costs associated with liquor, such as criminal prosecution and welfare, the residents of each county should be able to choose whether or not to license liquor sales within their borders. This effectively took away the right of municipalities to set their own liquor policy. When the newly elected legislature convened in early 1915, the option issue created a contentious, hard-fought political battle. Liquor interests and temperance advocates both used hardball tactics in an attempt to sway state legislators. The anti-saloon faction won. The Minnesota legislature passed the "County Option" law, meaning voters were empowered to ban liquor sales within their counties.[115] When the referendums were conducted, Steele County voters chose to allow liquor sales, while neighboring Dodge, Mower, and Freeborn Counties, all within a mile of Blooming Prairie, voted dry. Saloons in those counties were forced to close. The law had unintentionally created an opportunity for enterprising saloon keepers in wet coun-

115. William Lass, Minnesota: *A History*, New York: W.W. Norton, 1998, 215.

SALOONS HIT HARD BY ACTION OF PUBLIC SAFETY COMMISSION

Dancing and Cabaret Shows Under Ban—Women Barred From Cafes—New Closing and Opening Law to be Effective.

St. Paul, June 6.—The State Public Safety Commission in War Order No. 7, issued yesterday prohibits dancing and cabaret performances in any saloon or cafe, where liquor is sold, in the state; prohibits serving liquor to women and girls in any saloon or cafe in the cities over 50,000 population prohibits women from entering or receiving service from any saloon in the state.

The orders make the closing hour for all saloons and cafes, where liquor is sold, 10:00 p. m. instead of 11:00 p. m. and prohibits all saloons from being opened before 8:00 a. m.

Instructions are given to municipal government bodies to pass local legislation, conforming with the order, in which it is stipulated that the second violation of the order shall be punishable by revocation of license and imprisonment without the option of a fine.

The order is effective immediately.

Saloons were an early target of the Commission.
Daily People's Press, June 6th, 1917.

ties. The onset of war and the creation of a Commission with the power to regulate the liquor trade drastically changed the situation in Blooming Prairie.

Minnesotans generally supported the work of the Commission, and public support likely made it easier for the commission to impose its will in regulating the liquor trade, as the Blooming Prairie saloon keepers would learn.

Monday, July 1st, 1918, was a historic day in the annals of Blooming Prairie, Minnesota. That afternoon, Governor J.A.A. Burnquist, exasperated at the intransigence of Blooming Prairie saloon keepers and their defiance of state closing orders, ordered Brigadier General Walter F. Rhinow, commander of all Minnesota state troops, to close the saloons. The subsequent report detailed events:

> After repeated violation of an order of the Minnesota Commission of Public Safety regulating the hours of operation of the four saloons in the village of Blooming Prairie, Governor Burnquist ordered general Rhinow, on July 1st, 1918, to proceed at once with a detail of state troops and close up the saloons found operating in violation of the closing order. The order was received at 1:00 P.M. At 2:15 P.M. eight motor cars, furnished by the St. Paul battalion, Motor Corps, Minnesota Home Guard, left the State Capitol loaded with soldiers bound for Blooming Prairie. The run was made at a high rate of speed over good roads via Faribault and Owatonna.[116]

The result was an invasion of the village of Blooming Prairie; the first of two such events in 1918. On July 14th, the *Blooming Prairie Times* reported on the incident, "Adjutant General Rhinow, Lieutenant Glen Harrison and fifteen men of the First Minnesota Infantry arrived in town at 8:45 pm and ordered the saloons closed."

The troops remained outside the town while General Rhinow went into the village to survey the situation. Once Rhinow ascertained that the Blooming Prairie saloons were still operating, the

116. W.F. Rhinow, *Report of the Adjutant General of the State of Minnesota*, vol.1 Minneapolis: Syndicate Printing, 1918, 286.

troops were called into town, saloons were closed, and patrons were ordered out.

There was anger and reluctance to obey the order. In his report, Rhinow singled out saloon owner John Coggins for his obstinate behavior, saying, "They were ordered to close immediately, and all except the saloon owned and operated by John Coggins expressed their willingness to comply. He announced with much vehemence that he would remain open until he was closed. He was closed." [117]

Guards were posted at all entrances and remained on duty in Blooming Prairie for three weeks.[118] The saloon keepers still were not finished. They continued to find ways to sell liquor to their patrons. The situation was not fully resolved until October 1918.

In the normal course of events, it was extreme for the Governor and the National Guard to get involved in what would appear to be a local matter. However, in the case of the Blooming Prairie saloon keepers, local law enforcement was not enough. The bar owners "all but thumbed their noses" at the Steele County Sheriff and County Attorney. The County Sheriff claimed to have shut down the saloons three times to no avail.[119]

The saloon owners challenged the Governor's order in court. The legal challenge was especially important because it served as a test of Governor Burnquist's wartime power, as well as the power of the Public Safety Commission. The *Minneapolis Tribune* and other major Minnesota daily papers covered the story extensively.

There were many factors that played a role in the saloon keepers' rebellion. Temperance and prohibition had been a part of the political agenda for years, so many people supported the Commis-

117. Ibid., 286.

118. Ibid., 286.

119. Harold Severson, *Blooming Prairie Update* (Blooming Prairie: First National Bank of Blooming Prairie, 1980), 104.

sion. However, alcoholic beverages played a part in the culture and tradition of some groups. Blooming Prairie and the surrounding area had a large population of people with Irish or Bohemian ancestry. For many of them, and others (plenty of Norwegians liked to drink too), consumption in moderation of alcoholic beverages was a deeply ingrained part of their lives. Saloons could be places to meet friends and socialize. Drunkenness certainly occurred, but probably not to the extent portrayed by the Commission's stigmatizing propaganda. Furthermore, the saloon owners were engaged in a legal business, and they had families to feed. They needed to make a living.

There was one factor that thoroughly complicated the issue. The Blooming Prairie saloon keepers were in a unique geographic position that enabled them to make significant profits. They were distributing liquor into the dry counties, and northern Iowa. The Commission was determined to regulate the liquor trade and it had "near-dictatorial authority."[120]

The community of Blooming Prairie had about 1,000 residents in 1918. It was located in Steele County which was at the hub of four counties. Dodge County was just east of town, and Mower and Freeborn Counties lay to the south and west. The "Red Ball Highway," connected Blooming Prairie to the important economic hubs of Austin and Owatonna. West of town, the "Jefferson Highway" connected Blooming Prairie to Albert Lea, Minnesota and Mason City, Iowa.

The geographical location of Blooming Prairie is important because almost all the southern tier of counties in Minnesota, including Mower and Freeborn, were "dry" in the sense that no liquor sales were allowed. Individuals in dry counties could still possess and consume liquor purchased legally in a "wet" county. That

120. Blegen, *Minnesota: A History of the State.*

meant that the Blooming Prairie saloon keepers not only had a local market, but a large "dry" territory to service close to home. With the Iowa border being only about twenty-five miles south of Blooming Prairie, the saloon keepers also sold their liquor into "dry" portions of Northern Iowa. It was legal to sell liquor in Blooming Prairie; individuals could come into town and purchase for their own use. It is important to note however that it was not legal for a Blooming Prairie dealer to smuggle liquor into a dry county.

The Minnesota Commission of Public Safety was determined to regulate the liquor trade, and it was able to do so with its extraordinary dictatorial powers. The idea behind the Commission was that the state of Minnesota was vital, especially in terms of agricultural production and "indispensable iron ore."[121] Therefore, with American lives at stake, the government stepped in to stimulate production and suppress the things that might retard it. The Commission even used an old Vermont statute created in 1777 to justify its mandates. The Commission was created because of the wartime hysterics that swept Minnesota and the nation in 1917 and 1918. It had a wide range of oversight including agricultural production, alien registration, and the suppression of dissent. Among other things, controlling the liquor trade was high on its agenda. Ultimately, the Commission issued 59 orders during its existence and 21 of these dealt exclusively with the liquor trade. Three of the 21 were specifically addressed to the saloon keepers of Blooming Prairie.[122]

Local newspapers raised the issue of the Blooming Prairie liquor trade in June 1917. In a long, scathing editorial, the Albert Lea Tribune placed the blame for accidents on area highways squarely on "wet" voters in Owatonna, Steele County, and Blooming Prairie.

121. Burnquist et al. *Report of Minnesota Commission of Public Safety*, 10.

122. Ibid., 125-126.

The newspaper went so far as to accuse Blooming Prairie "wets" of "putting terror in those who travel 'the fine Red Ball route' through that place to Austin and Mason City." The logic was, if picnickers could not travel in safety to area parks, merchants suffered as no money was spent. The editorial called for a record to be kept on persistent offenders and taking steps to control their actions. It concluded with this paragraph:

> How many people will it be necessary to maim or kill and how much property must be sacrificed before something is done to protect travelers on the crowded hiway? [sic]

The pressure was on. People outside of Blooming Prairie noticed the problem of the Blooming Prairie liquor trade and called for action to bring it under control. On September 30, 1917, the *Owatonna Journal-Chronicle* reported that Austin City Attorney, J.N. Nicholson; along with E.N. Hoffman, a lawyer from Blooming Prairie, petitioned the Public Safety Commission to order the closing of four saloons and three wholesale liquor establishments in Blooming Prairie. The attorney cited as precedent, "Commission order number ten issued September 17th, 1917, which had regulated liquor sales in Martin and Pipestone Counties."[123] The problem was not only disorder in Blooming Prairie, it was the large shipment of liquor into "dry" counties. The Austin Police Chief was arresting many people bringing liquor into Austin and Mower County.

As 1917 wore on, the Commission was busy organizing, spreading into every County and Township, issuing numerous regulatory orders, delineating the price of milk and the sale of bread,

123. Ibid., 30-31.

organizing a Home Guard to replace the National Guard and, of course, regulating the liquor trade. By December of 1917, the Commission's September petition regarding Blooming Prairie saloons was partially successful. In a very broad finding on December 5th, 1917 the Commission blamed Blooming Prairie merchants' sale of intoxicating liquors for interfering with the production of food and damaging the health and good habits of soldiers of both the national army and state militia in the area. The finding went so far as to blame Blooming Prairie liquor for interfering with the successful prosecution of the war between the United States and Germany. Order number seventeen stated:

> "That the sale of intoxicating liquors as it has been and is being conducted in the village of Blooming Prairie aforesaid has interfered and is interfering with the production of food and with the health and good habits of the soldiers of the national army and of the militia in the territory adjacent to said Village, and that it has interfered and is interfering with the efficiency of the application of the military civil and industrial resources of the states of Minnesota and Iowa towards the maintenance of the defense of the said states and the nation . . .[124]

If true, those offences would be serious and almost treasonous. The Commission cited no evidence for such sweeping charges; nevertheless, they were determined to constrict the Blooming Prairie liquor trade. They ordered saloon keepers to sell only at retail and only between the hours of 9:00 a.m. and 5:00 p.m. Furthermore,

---

124. Burnquist et al. *Report of Minnesota Commission of Public Safety*, 90-91.

no liquor could be taken out of a saloon and violators could lose their right to sell liquor. The Steele County Sheriff was charged with serving the order.[125]

The order, if obeyed, would have solved several problems in the eyes of the Commission. "Dry" counties would stay dry, highways would be safe, and comity with the state of Iowa would be restored. There was a report in the December 7th, 1917 edition of the *Owatonna Journal-Chronicle* of Iowa tourists to Blooming Prairie making the highways dangerous by returning home drunk. It must be noted here that transporting liquor into "dry" areas was not illegal in 1917. Law enforcement officers and citizens often disapproved, but it was legal. That would change in May of 1918.

Interestingly, given all the publicity about the problems in Blooming Prairie, the majority of Blooming Prairie and Owatonna citizens voted "wet" in the local March 1918 elections. The mayoral race in Blooming Prairie was an exception with the "dry" candidate winning. On the issue of liquor licenses, the "wets" prevailed in Blooming Prairie by 32 votes and in Owatonna by 108.

In early May 1918, the Blooming Prairie saloon keepers challenged Commission Order 17. On Wednesday, May 1st, three of the four Blooming Prairie saloons were open after 5:00 p.m. Blooming Prairie mayor H.H. Willberg had learned of the saloon keepers' intentions and was ready with a notice that was served on the proprietors shortly after 5:00 p.m. The notice reminded the saloon owners of the terms of Order 17 and the consequences of violating that order. Mayor Willberg, "dry," called the Blooming Prairie village council together to consider the matter. According to the *Blooming Prairie Times*, the council ("wet") declined to address the issue on the grounds that it properly belonged to the Public Safety Commission.

125. Ibid.

The Commission responded quickly, issuing Order 34 on May 14th, 1918:

> Whereas, P.P. Coggins, Geo. E. Thomas, and W.R. Carroll are operating saloons in the Village of Blooming Prairie, Steele County, Minnesota, in violation and defiance of law, and of the commission's Order Number 17.
>
> The President of said Village is directed and ordered to close said saloons forthwith for and during the period of the war, using all lawful means to that end.
>
> And said P.P. Coggins. Geo. E. Thomas and W.R. Carroll are prohibited from engaging, directly or in the business of selling intoxicating liquor in said Village during the period of the war.
>
> Dated at St. Paul, Minnesota, May 14th, 1918.
> MINNESOTA COMMISSION OF PUBLIC SAFETY
> J.A.A. Burnquist,
> Governor and ex-officio Chairman.[126]

The Commission was not finished. That same day, May 14th, 1918, Commissioners issued Order 35, a sweeping regulation that prohibited the transport of liquor into and through dry districts. The order asserted that the transport made highways dangerous, spread disorder and "diminished the efficiency of the man-power of the state in exploiting resources needed by the nation." The single exception was steam railroads transporting liquor into Minnesota.

---

126. Burnquist et al. *Report of Minnesota Commission of Public Safety,* 116.

Any peace officer was authorized to halt vehicles, provided the officer had reasonable grounds to suspect liquor was being moved. Any liquor found was to be seized and disposed of.[127]

Battle lines were drawn. Convinced they operated legitimate businesses, the tenacious saloon owners defied the Commission. It was at this time the Steele County Sheriff came to Blooming Prairie with orders from Governor Burnquist and closed the saloons. However, the saloons reopened. On May 16th, 1918, The *Blooming Prairie Times* noted ominously that " . . . it would not be surprising if the Commission should resort to drastic action to force compliance with its orders."

The saloon owners' next step was to take the issue to court. Because of a change of venue, the case was heard in Hennepin County. By then, and perhaps because of the legal implications, newspapers outside the local area were covering the case.

At first, saloon keeper William R. Carroll obtained a temporary restraining order against the Commission, and the saloons reopened on June 7th, 1918. However, the *Blooming Prairie Times* reported that, on June 22nd, Hennepin County District Court Judge W.E. Hale ordered Steele County Sheriff Leehy to close the saloons again. Sheriff Leehy served notice that any effort to reopen would be dealt with sternly. The saloons were to remain closed until a trial could be held on the merits of the restraining order. Sheriff Leehy claimed to have closed the saloons on three occasions, but the saloons continued to reopen until Governor Burnquist sent in the militia to close them and stand guard until the issue could be decided in court. Blooming Prairie citizens treated the soldiers courteously. The legal case was postponed until late July of 1918, when it reached the Supreme Court of Minnesota. The case was initially expected to define the powers of the Minne-

127. Ibid.

sota Public Safety Commission, as well as those of the Governor as head of the Commission. On June 27th, the *Blooming Prairie Times* reported that another Blooming Prairie saloon keeper, George Thomas, was arrested near Northwood, Iowa about thirty miles southwest of Blooming Prairie. He was caught transferring 200 quarts of whiskey from his car to a railroad handcar heading south. The county sheriff had been tipped off the supply was destined for Mason City, Iowa. It turned out to be an expensive day for Thomas. He pled guilty to charges of illegal transport of liquor, delivered the whiskey for destruction, and paid a fine of $100.

In early August of 1918, the Supreme Court of Minnesota ruled on the Blooming Prairie case. The court ruled that Governor Burnquist was acting constitutionally when he ordered the closure of the saloons. The court did not rule on the validity of the Commission's orders, only that Burnquist was doing his duty as Governor. That should have ended the whole affair. The saloon keepers had been closed repeatedly by local authorities and finally by the state militia, yet they refused to give up.

The situation in Blooming Prairie reached a climax in late September. On September 24th, 1918, the Commission issued its final order, Order Number 48, regarding the saloons. Liquor licenses were revoked, liquor was to be removed or confiscated within ten days, and the Governor was to enforce the order. Several Blooming Prairie citizens signed affidavits swearing that liquor was still being sold. The Commission decided it was time to "clean house" in Blooming Prairie. On the evening of Friday, September 27th, Special Agent L.J. Glaeser arrived in town with twenty deputies in eight cars of the Motor Reserve Corps. It was the second invasion of Blooming Prairie in less than three months. Guards were placed at saloons, and saloon keepers and the mayor were served with the Commission's latest order. Coggins' saloon was locked; however, voices and clinking glasses were heard from the outside. Guards forced open the main door, Coggins interfered, and was knocked down. That was the last of any direct clashes with state officials, at least in Blooming Prairie. At first, the saloon owners claimed to have no outside stocks of liquor, but raids on warehouses revealed large quantities stored; an estimated eight thousand dollars worth. It was all resold to parties outside of Blooming Prairie, in "wet" areas of Minnesota.

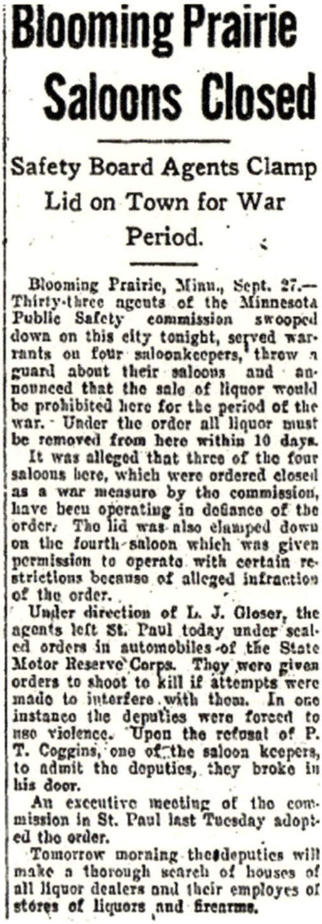

Blooming Prairie Saloons Closed

Safety Board Agents Clamp Lid on Town for War Period.

Blooming Prairie, Minn., Sept. 27.—Thirty-three agents of the Minnesota Public Safety commission swooped down on this city tonight, served warrants on four saloonkeepers, threw a guard about their saloons and announced that the sale of liquor would be prohibited here for the period of the war. Under the order all liquor must be removed from here within 10 days.

It was alleged that three of the four saloons here, which were ordered closed as a war measure by the commission, have been operating in defiance of the order. The lid was also clamped down on the fourth saloon which was given permission to operate with certain restrictions because of alleged infraction of the order.

Under direction of L. J. Gloser, the agents left St. Paul today under sealed orders in automobiles of the State Motor Reserve Corps. They were given orders to shoot to kill if attempts were made to interfere with them. In one instance the deputies were forced to use violence. Upon the refusal of P. T. Coggins, one of the saloon keepers, to admit the deputies, they broke in his door.

An executive meeting of the commission in St. Paul last Tuesday adopted the order.

Tomorrow morning the deputies will make a thorough search of houses of all liquor dealers and their employes of stores of liquors and firearms.

Front page news,
the Commission cracked down!
Minneapolis Tribune, September 28th, 1918.

Blooming Prairie Main Street entrance to what was Coggins' saloon.
Photo by Dean Ulland.

Glaeser and his men abused their authority during the episode. They stopped many young men in the area and detained some for failing to produce their draft cards. Those actions cost Agent Glaeser his job. He was dismissed by the Commission and replaced by a Minneapolis deputy. The crackdown continued in the area for several days, resulting in a large quantity of liquor being seized from bootleggers headed to Iowa. In one case, the use of firearms was necessary to stop a driver. In the village of Geneva, in "dry" Freeborn County, not far from Blooming Prairie, a "blind pig" (or speakeasy) was raided and the liquor confiscated.

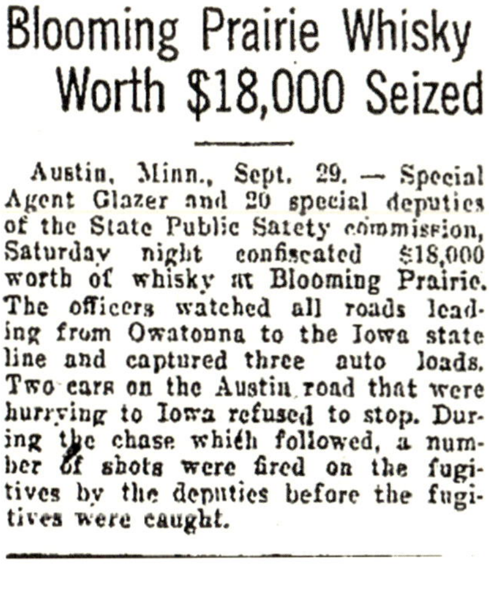

Blooming Prairie Whisky Worth $18,000 Seized

Austin, Minn., Sept. 29. — Special Agent Glazer and 20 special deputies of the State Public Safety commission, Saturday night confiscated $18,000 worth of whisky at Blooming Prairie. The officers watched all roads leading from Owatonna to the Iowa state line and captured three auto loads. Two cars on the Austin road that were hurrying to Iowa refused to stop. During the chase which followed, a number of shots were fired on the fugitives by the deputies before the fugitives were caught.

"Blooming Prairie Whiskey Worth $18,000 Seized"
Minneapolis Tribune, September 29th, 1918.

"Green River: The Whiskey Without a Headache" Pre-Prohibition whiskey, likely purchased in Blooming Prairie.
Dean Ulland, private collection.

The *Blooming Prairie Times* reported on October 10th, 1918, "Town Now Bone Dry." By order of the Commission, Blooming Prairie would stay dry until three months after ratification of peace with Germany.

With Blooming Prairie dry at last, many citizens were satisfied, and having their day in court seemed to placate some the saloon keepers. However, the episode split the community. Some citizens were disgruntled by what they saw as the Commission's heavy hand. For a time, Blooming Prairie had been a major bootlegging center in Minnesota and would be again during the Prohibition Era a few years later. The saloon keepers were simply supplying the demand for liquor. Blooming Prairie's geographical position relative to the "dry" areas of southern Minnesota and northern Iowa created substantial opportunity. A well-intended law allowing the local option on alcohol sales, combined with the actions of the Minnesota Commission of Public Safety unintentionally created criminals out of the Blooming Prairie saloon keepers.

Nationwide prohibition went into effect in January 1920. The era of saloons on mainstreet was gone.

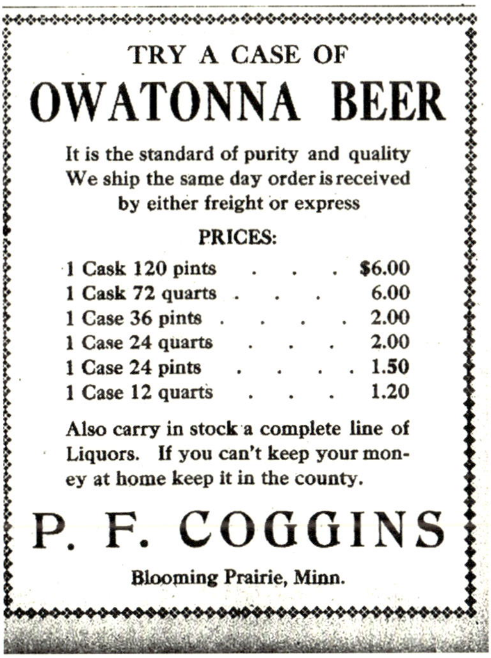

Beer prices in 1917.
People's Press, April 17th, 1917.

9

DISSENT, DISLOYALTY, AND POLITICS

"There are during this war but two parties, one the loyalists, the other the disloyalists."
—Minnesota Governor J.A.A. Burnquist

"Now that we have a price set on sisal hemp, it is to be hoped that some Minnesota politicians will soon reach the end of their ropes."
—*The Nonpartisan Leader,*
March 25th, 1918

Questions about the right to dissent and what constituted disloyalty were inextricably linked to wartime politics. They could not be separated. Both the state and federal government passed draconian laws that sharply curtailed American's constitutional rights, and for the most part, Americans supported them. In Minnesota, those questions were especially important during the election year of 1918.

The political arena is never for the fainthearted, and in 1918, that was especially true of the Republican gubernatorial primary.

The election pitted former sixth district Congressman Charles A. Lindbergh Sr. (the famous aviator's father) against sitting Republican Governor J.A.A. Burnquist. Given the passions aroused by the war, it is not surprising that it was a bitter, hard-fought contest. Lindbergh's opposition to the war was an endless source of controversy as his campaign moved across the state.

Lindbergh, a Republican endorsed by the NPL, was opposed to American entry into the war. While he believed the American cause was just because of German depredations on the high seas, he still thought the American decision for war unwise, saying: "I believe the problem could have been settled without war or sacrifice of national honor, the same as we expect to adjust the trespass upon our rights to the high seas by other nations."[128]

We know about the brave young men and women who served in the armed forces or otherwise found themselves in harm's way, sometimes working as nurses or American Field Service ambulance drivers. We know about the many people who contributed financially to the war effort, albeit with varying levels of enthusiasm, and of course, the volunteers who devoted countless hours to the war effort. However, there is another, more intolerant part of the wartime experience to be considered. Citizens were quick to turn on their neighbors, especially if they had a suspicious ethnic (usually German) background or supported "radical" organizations like the IWW or NPL. Accusations of disloyalty or being a "slacker" were hurled with impunity. Newspapers almost seemed to be an arm of the state, willing to engage in public humiliation based on the slimmest of evidence. The *Austin Weekly Herald* was especially bad in that regard, going so far as to publish at least one unsigned letter to the editor. Then there were the vigilantes. Reports of their

128. Lindbergh Charles A., *Your Country at War and What Happens to you After a War* (Philadelphia, Dorrance and Company, 1934), 16.

misdeeds, sometimes criminal or even life-threatening in nature, were often ignored by law enforcement authorities.

Other chapters in this work describe the coercion that took place in Liberty Bond and other fund drives. Those incidents were only part of the story. A closer look at other aspects of Minnesotan's lives reveals just how far the judicial, and political systems went to enforce their version of "loyalty," sometimes to the extent of tolerating, and even encouraging, vigilante activities. To be sure, other states had extreme cases of intolerance and authoritarianism, but Minnesota was among the worst. It is fair to say that, while thousands of young Minnesotans went off to war, Minnesota state and local governments sometimes went to war against their own citizens. Even the Federal government recognized it. Yet most Minnesotans supported such actions. Looking at it a century later, their conduct can be hard to understand.

Those who challenged the status quo faced a wide variety of legal and extra-legal measures designed to force them into line. Minnesotans across the state and in Mower, Freeborn, and Steele Counties experienced the intolerant underside of patriotism.

The rights enshrined in the First Amendment are tantamount aspects of American identity. The amendment guarantees the right to assemble and speak without fear of retribution from the government. Americans enjoy the benefits of a free press, and the freedom to worship as they choose. It protects the Republic and contains perhaps the most important words in the Constitution. The first amendment is the essence of freedom—or is it? When President Wilson sought a declaration of war against Germany in 1917, he justified it by saying, "the world must be made safe for democracy." Ironically, in 1917-18 Wilson, Congress, and millions of Americans, including many in Minnesota, were willing to sacrifice democracy at home in the process of saving it for the world.

Because of its guarantee of free speech, it is reasonable to assume that newspapers would be among the First Amendment's most ardent defenders. That was not always the case. On July 6th, 1917, the editor of the *Austin Weekly Herald* called for censorship. A short comment in the "Pot Pourri" section, presumably written, or approved, by the publishers John and Gertrude Skinner said this: "A few of the newspapers are complaining of the censorship which has been established by the government. When our soldier's lives are at stake, we should be able to suppress our curiosity. News of importance will keep."

Monday April 8th, 1918, was special in Austin. It was Governor's Day, and the *Mower County Transcript-Republican* reporter was at his colorful best in describing the afternoon: "Every heart was throbbing with patriotism as the sun came up over the eastern horizon and the mist clouds began to scatter." Governor Burnquist was coming to town during a bitter Republican primary campaign. A special car on the noon train brought Governor and Mrs. Burnquist along with their party to Austin. Community leaders had organized a busy afternoon and evening of receptions and speeches, culminating in a dinner for the assorted dignitaries and a Red Cross ball at the armory.

It was a beautiful early spring day; flags were fluttering in the breeze, and Austin was crowded. People were visiting Austin from all over the county, excited about the day's festivities. Most stores across the county were closed, and all Mower County schools were asked to declare a half-holiday so schoolchildren could witness the patriotic event. As a result, Austin streets were a "throbbing mass of humanity."

There was a variety of entertainment. Minnesota Home Guard Company C, composed of the Austin unit, and auxiliary units from Adams, Brownsdale, Dexter, Grand Meadow, Lyle, Le-

Roy, Taopi, and Rose Creek, 450 men in all, participated in drills. The Austin second platoon showed off their skills in French bayonet work, and the guardsmen from Lyle group demonstrated their proficiency in quelling street riots. The local units each seemed to have some specialty. When the drilling was done, all units passed in front of a reviewal stand on Main Street, where they received the Governor's salute.

Burnquist's "patriotic address" opening the Third Liberty Loan campaign was the highlight of the celebration. Thousands lined the streets. In his speech, Burnquist's uncompromising attitude toward disloyalty was on full display

"I would rather lose my position, all I possess or hope to possess, or life itself than be accused of disloyalty and bring disgrace on my children for generations to come." Strong words, but Burnquist was not done. "If anyone comes to this country, enjoys its privileges, its franchise, takes advantage of the opportunities afforded by the American flag and then is disloyal, he should be deprived of his franchise, have his property confiscated and be deported."

Noble sentiments, maybe, but what exactly, did it mean to be disloyal? Governor Burnquist was sure that he knew. Furthermore, as his speech indicated, he was willing to go to extreme lengths to enforce his vision of loyalty. The enforcement arm was the Minnesota Commission of Public Safety (the Commission). As discussed elsewhere in this volume, the Commission had a broad mandate. Part of that mandate was the suppression of disloyalty. The Commission's final report, issued at war's end, defined both loyalty and disloyalty. They described a loyal person in wartime as someone who is "wholeheartedly for the war and subordinates everything else to its successful prosecution."[129] Vague, to be sure, so was their definition of disloyalty. It meant in the Commission's (and Burn-

129. Burnquist et al. R*eport of Minnesota Commission of Public Safety*, 31.

quist's) view, those who misinterpreted "the constitutional guarantee of freedom of speech and press." That, of course, could mean anything, but their focus was on three groups of people.

The first targeted group was "professional and theoretical pacifists." In other words, anti-war activists. There were some anti-war groups in Minnesota and nationwide.[130]

The second group in their sights were "men of pro-German traditions and sympathies," or people with family and sentimental ties to Germany. Understandably, some of them were reluctant to take up arms against Germany. The report indicates that they focused on Minnesota River Valley communities, especially New Ulm, which was home to many Minnesotans of German heritage. Ethnic Germans were considered suspect everywhere in Minnesota.[131]

The Commission's third target was "professional politicians of a socialist or Nonpartisan League stamp who sought to win votes at their country's cost by pandering to a treasonable sentiment."[132]

Most Minnesotans, caught up in wartime frenzy, agreed with Burnquist and the Commission. That was the secret to their success. Most citizens agreed or were at least willing to acquiesce in the suppression of any activity that met their definition of disloyalty. Government agencies did not do it alone. There was always active citizen participation. A century later, it is surprising to see how many Minnesotans looked the other way as their traditional rights and liberties were ignored.

In December 1917, Dexter area farmer John Christgau journeyed to Austin and stopped his subscription to the *Austin Weekly Herald*. Christgau, a naturalized citizen, born in Germany, was angry with the paper's pro-war editorial stance and he was not afraid

130. Ibid.

131. Ibid.

132. Ibid.

to make his feelings known. He also registered his disgust with University of Minnesota president Marion Burton's comment that he "would do his damndest [sic] to make sure slackers did their duty." Christgau's comments earned him a scolding in a front page "above the fold" article. The *Herald* noted that Christgau was fortunate. Because he had a loyal brother, and two loyal sons already drafted and serving in the army no one had turned him into the Public Safety Commission.

Fred W. Schmidt, an Alden Township farmer, was not so lucky. In May 1918, District Court Judge S.D. Catherwood "administered a severe lecture," sentenced him to 6 months in jail (suspended), and fined him $500, a huge sum in 1918 (about $8,500 dollars in 2021). It was Schmidt's punishment for making "seditious remarks." According to the County Attorney, the statements he made included, "The United States has a rotten government" and that "he didn't care which side won the war." Feelings ran so high at the hearing that Schmidt had an exceedingly difficult time finding an attorney to represent him. Attorney H.A. Morgan asked to be excused on the grounds that he didn't want to represent a pro-German. Finally, Probate Court Judge Mayland agreed to take the job and after a short conference, the defendant pled guilty. A report on the matter in the May 16th, 1918, *Freeborn County Standard* concluded by noting, "it is the consensus of opinion of the community that the fine and sentence was a light one and that Schmidt was lucky to escape a term in jail." This happened despite the fact Schmidt had purchased a liberty bond in the second drive.

Christgau and Schmidt are just two examples of people punished in some way for expressing their opinions: Christgau by publicly humiliation and Schmidt by the legal system. By speaking out, both men ran afoul of Federal and State laws enacted during the wartime hysteria of 1917-18, laws that seemed to ignore the basic rights of a free people, especially those rights enshrined in the 1st Amendment. Perhaps even worse than breaking the law, their actions offended the sensibilities of their neighbors.

There are many other examples of local citizens caught up in the hysterical atmosphere of wartime Minnesota. Sometimes their "crimes" seem minor, but whatever the offence, the punishment was at the very least an embarrassing episode in the life of the supposed miscreant.

Theodore Nelson, described as an Albert Lea real estate businessman, was accused by Mrs. Ruth Jensen of "seditious utterances." Mr. Nelson is supposed to have stated that a Red Cross fund-raising auction was "humbug," along with making other disloyal statements of a serious nature.

The charge was taken seriously. Apparently, Nelson had a reputation of being an "anti," against whatever the issue happened to be, leaving people with the impression he was pro-German. He had, in fact, spoken out in opposition to American entry in the war. That did not make him pro-German. He pointed out in his defense that his son was serving his country in Battery A. The case had to be postponed three times because no Albert Lea lawyer would defend Nelson. He was eventually able to procure the services of Owatonna attorney A.W. Sawyer. It did not matter. Freeborn County Attorney Peterson and Mrs. Jensen prevailed. Sawyer's efforts to protect his client's legal and constitutional rights came to nothing.

Mrs. Jensen, County Attorney Peterson, and Freeborn County Judge Hammond all believed their version of "patriotism" outweighed Nelson's right to due process and the rule of law. Nelson's chosen humiliation, forced to publicly kiss the flag, was a message to all citizens. The Nelson case merited a long, front page article in the March 25th, 1918, edition of the *Freeborn County Standard* announced: "Theodore Nelson, arrested on the complaint of disloyalty, publicly kissed the United states flag Monday afternoon in Albert Lea before Judge Hammond, the attorneys and a large crowd at the city hall." The resounding message was whatever doubts you might have about the war: KEEP YOUR MOUTH SHUT. Steele, Freeborn, and Mower County newspapers covered the case extensively. It was a bad day for Nelson and the rule of law.

Another example of a citizen running afoul of a local zealot involved a Hayward man, and it made the front page of the April 1st, 1918, *Freeborn County Standard*:

> Henry Kampmeyer was arrested Saturday by Sheriff Fosse and brought to this city, charged with making seditious statements. The complaintant [sic] is Louis H. Kuchera, also living near Hayward. The defendant is charged with making the following serious and seditious remarks against the conduct of the war: "The United States has no business in this war. She was the one that made this war against the Germans. The selective draft, which is in use by our government is no better than the German military system." Kampmeyer was taken before the court in the afternoon and the hearing was continued till Tuesday morning. Bail was fixed at $1,000, and the bond was signed by Jim Kipra of Hayward.

At the behest of Governor Burnquist and his desire to enforce "100 percent loyalty," the Minnesota Legislature acted quickly. Within two weeks of U.S. entry into the war, the Minnesota Sedition Act was approved, and legislation setting up the Commission of Public Safety was enacted.[133]

The Sedition Act preceded a similar Federal law by two months. The law made it illegal to print, publish, circulate, or advocate in public before more than five persons that men should not enlist in the armed forces or that citizens should not aid or assist the United States government in carrying on war.[134]

When taken in conjunction with the extremely broad powers of the Commission, "to do all acts and things non-inconsistent with the Constitution or laws of the State of Minnesota or of the United States, which are necessary or proper for the public safety and for the protection of life and public property or private property . . . " including, "The Suppression of Disloyalty."[135] Minnesotan's freedom to express themselves was restricted.

By June 1917, the Commission was organized at the county and precinct level. For example, in Steele County, Thomas Cashman issued the call for patriotic citizens to meet and organize. Rules were set out; it was a formal process. On June 19th, *The Daily People's Press* reported on it in detail:

> The following rules of the Public Safety Commission are to be borne in mind: Article 2 of the proposed articles of the Association states that the purpose of the Association shall be to assist the Minnesota Public Safety Commission in the work provided for said commission under and by virtue of the Laws of Minnesota. In Article 3 each person irrespective of age and sex in said County who loves America and

133. Carol E. Jenson, "Loyalty as a Political Weapon: The 1918 Campaign in Minnesota." *Minnesota History*, Spring, 1972, 44.

134. Ibid.

135. Burnquist et al. *Report of Minnesota Commission of Public Safety*, 7.

> respects its institutions shall be eligible for membership in the Association. "The precinct meeting will be open to all. Every precinct will elect five delegates and all the citizens of the county are invited to attend the general meeting which will be held June 30th. Local meetings for the election of the delegates by the several towns and villages will be held in the voting precincts where the general election was held in November 1916. In the towns the meetings shall be called to order by the Chairman of the Town Board. In the villages the meetings shall be called to order by the President.

The local Public Safety Commision (PSC) organizations were extensive. Townships, villages, and cities across the state had many citizens participating in Commission activities, at least on paper. Everyone kept an eye on their neighbors.

In Freeborn County, the *Freeborn County Standard* reported on March 7th, 1918 that "Jim McQuire of Twin Lakes is loyal all the way through and he is going to see that every man in his neighborhood, Twin Lakes, is the same. Jim is a member of Company D of the Home Guard and intends to use his official capacity to enforce his intentions. It was noised around that Nonpartisan organizers were secretly planning a meeting at the town hall at Twin Lakes last Saturday night to extract $16.00 apiece from some of the farmers thereabouts. Jim and several of his friends got wind of the fact and started preparations for a reception. Tar, of the old-fashioned variety, was procured and an ancient feather bed was obtained." The "organizers" were evidently tipped off and the meeting never came to pass.

On March 3rd, 1918, the Postmaster of Alden heard of an upcoming meeting of the NPL to be held at a schoolhouse in Mansfield township. He notified Martin Blacklin, Freeborn County director of the PSC. Blacklin in turn notified the Freeborn County Attorney and the Captain of the Home Guard. They stopped the meeting. Reports indicate that "rather than make the occasion a complete loss, the NPL took up a collection for the Red Cross." [136]

The federal government also enacted legislation aimed at suppressing dissent. In June of 1917, Congress passed the Espionage Act. Amended in May of 1918, the Act made it a Federal crime to use profane, disloyal, abusive or scurrilous speech about the U.S. government, the U.S. flag, or the uniform of the army and navy. The Postmaster General could impound publications in violation of the Act.

In two short months, state and federal law had made the "land of the free" decidedly less so. There were limits beyond which Americans could not go without facing vigorous prosecution. Those limits seem contrary to the First Amendment:

> "Congress shall make no law respecting an establishment of religion, or prohibiting the free exercise thereof; or abridging the freedom of speech, or of the press; or the right of the people peaceably to assemble, and to petition the Government for a redress of grievances."[137]

Politics, law, and vigilantism all came together in the primary campaign of 1918. Minnesota had never seen a campaign like it, especially in a primary. To say that the statewide campaign was

136. Carol E. Jenson, *Agrarian Pioneer in Civil Liberties: The Nonpartisan League in Minnesota During World War I.* (New York: Garland, 1986), 94.

137. "Amendment I" https://www.constituteproject.org.

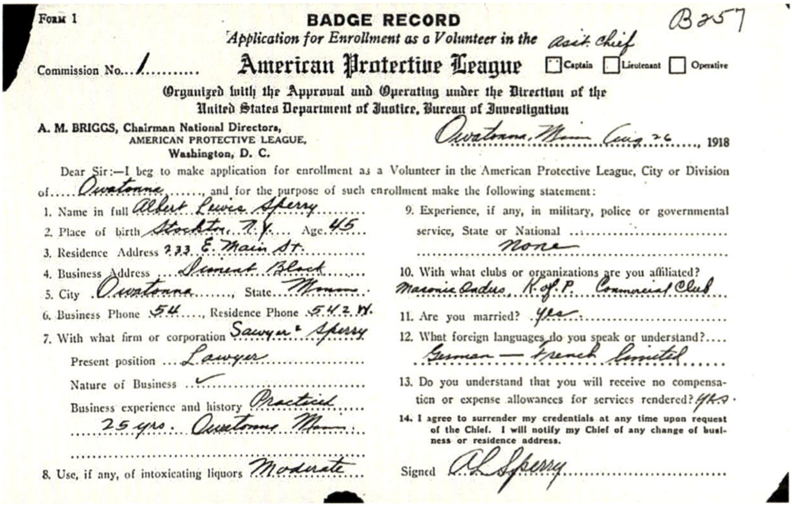
FORM 1 BADGE RECORD B257

Application for Enrollment as a Volunteer in the Ass't Chief

Commission No. 1 American Protective League ☐ Captain ☐ Lieutenant ☐ Operative

Organized with the Approval and Operating under the Direction of the United States Department of Justice, Bureau of Investigation

A. M. BRIGGS, Chairman National Directors,
AMERICAN PROTECTIVE LEAGUE,
Washington, D. C.

Owatonna, Minn Aug 26, 1918

Dear Sir:—I beg to make application for enrollment as a Volunteer in the American Protective League, City or Division of Owatonna, and for the purpose of such enrollment make the following statement:

1. Name in full Albert Lewis Sperry
2. Place of birth Stockton N.Y. Age 45
3. Residence Address 233 E. Main St.
4. Business Address Dennent Block
5. City Owatonna, State Minn
6. Business Phone 54, Residence Phone 542 W.
7. With what firm or corporation Sawyer & Sperry
   Present position Lawyer
   Nature of Business ✓
   Business experience and history Practiced 25 yrs. Owatonna Minn.
8. Use, if any, of intoxicating liquors Moderate
9. Experience, if any, in military, police or governmental service, State or National None
10. With what clubs or organizations are you affiliated? Masonic Orders, K. of P. Commercial Club
11. Are you married? Yes
12. What foreign languages do you speak or understand? German — French limited
13. Do you understand that you will receive no compensation or expense allowances for services rendered? Yes.
14. I agree to surrender my credentials at any time upon request of the Chief. I will notify my Chief of any change of business or residence address.

Signed A L Sperry

Owatonna Attorney Albert Sperry's enrollment application for the American Protective League.
Public domain image.

hard-fought is an understatement and southern Minnesota was no exception. Local connections and candidates make the 1918 primary especially interesting and worth recalling in detail. The primary election was held on June 17th, 1918. Minnesotans turned out in record numbers to support Governor Burnquist, the Republican on the ticket. The headline following the primary was, "Freeborn County Remains Loyal," in the June 20th, 1918 edition of the *Freeborn County Standard*. The article went on to define loyalty as "standing solidly behind the state government and its war acts."

The primary election was hotly contested. The NPL's strategy was to challenge Republican party establishment figures in the primary, rather than create party machinery of their own. The NPL was not on the ballot as a separate party. It was a strange election. The Nonpartisan Leaguers ran as Republicans, even though their platform was far to the left of traditional Republican ideology. Incumbent

The NPL endorsed Lindbergh.
The Nonpartisan Leader, May 6th, 1918.

Republican Governor Burnquist was forced to contest a position that, given his popularity, should have been his by acclamation.

Again and again, we come across the term "NPL" in accounts of Minnesota politics 1917-1918. Local newspapers frequently criticized this group. In the minds of many Minnesotans, the term was synonymous with disloyalty, as bad as being pro-German. Just what was the NPL, and how did the organization acquire such a bad reputation?

The Nonpartisan League, usually referred to as the NPL, was a farm organization/political party founded in 1915 by North Dakota flax farmer Arthur C. Townley. He established the NPL after suffering financial ruin as a result of a failed crop. He blamed his plight partly on market speculators and set about recruiting like-minded farmers for his new group. In some ways, the NPL was a rebirth of the agrarian populist politics that attracted many great plains farmers in the 1880s and especially the 1890s. It sprang from a deep-seated anger at the "interests." In the minds of North Dakotans, that meant Minneapolis banks, grain millers, and shippers. They were accused by many farmers (with some justification) of manipulating weights, grades, and shipping rates. In other words, ruthless exploitation. The NPL was radical in the sense that its platform called for some socialistic measures to address the problems. The NPL called for a state-owned bank and grain elevator, as well as a state-owned railroad (even in 2020, North Dakota has a state-owned bank and elevator). They also called for a graduated income tax and other progressive measures designed to help farmers and labor.

The NPL was successful in North Dakota. It controlled the legislature following the 1916 elections, and the NPL candidate was easily elected governor. Political control there meant much of the NPL platform was, over time, adopted. Townley, sensing an opportunity to expand his movement, started promoting the NPL in

Satan Rebuking Sin.

Of all the crust ever displayed that man A. C. Townley of the Non (?) Partisan league has the "crustiest" crust! Think of him—he—A. C. Townley demanding that Judge McGee be removed from the Minnesota Safety commission! Townley! We wouldn't be any more surprised if we were to hear of a notorious bandit demanding the removal of the sheriff from a county before his gang drove in and robbed the bank! Not a bit! The patriotic people of Minnesota demand the removal of C. A. Townley to some isolated quarter until after the war has been won.—Albert Lea Times-Enterprise.

Princeton Union, May 16th, 1918.

Minnesota and other Great Plains and midwestern states. National headquarters were established in St. Paul.

At first, NPL organizing in Minnesota did not attract much attention. In fact, some communities cooperated by providing facilities for meetings. It was good for business. However, as NPL strength grew, so did opposition. As we have seen, Minnesotans at war were an intolerant bunch and, among other things, the NPL was perceived to be anti-war. Consequently, it was viewed as a disloyal group. Despite Townley's frequent statements of loyalty, and support for the war, NPL activities were viewed with suspicion and often outright hostility. The association with socialism hurt too. Many socialists, like Eugene Debs, were anti-war. In fact, Debs was eventually tried, convicted, and imprisoned for urging Americans to resist the draft. Sometimes, the NPL was accused of being tied to the Industrial Workers of the World (IWW). The "Wobblies," as they were colloquially termed, was a radical labor union that sometimes even turned violent.

One other association meant trouble for the NPL. Many Minnesotans of German heritage supported them. The NPL was the only political group that would listen to German experiences. It was a "voice for the voiceless," and during the war, German-Minnesotans did not have a voice in the mainstream Republican and Democrat parties. They found their voice in the NPL. As a result, several Minnesota counties with large German populations supported Lindbergh, not Burnquist, in the 1918 Republican primary. Lindbergh carried Brown County (the New Ulm area), Sibley, Carver, and Stearns (St. Cloud) Counties by significant margins.

Locally, the NPL was crushed. In Freeborn, Mower, and Steele Counties, incumbent Governor Burnquist easily defeated Lindbergh. However, townships with large German populations often voted the NPL slate. In Mower County, Adams and Waltham townships, both with significant German populations did just that. Frankford and Udolpho townships in Mower County also voted NPL, but for different reasons.

In Steele County, overall results were the same with Burnquist coasting to victory. Still, Meriden, Lemond, and Aurora townships were Lindbergh country, and several other townships were close.

In Freeborn County, Lindbergh was trounced by a 3-1 margin. He was especially unpopular in the villages. Glenville, Emmons, Geneva, Alden, and Hartland cast a grand total of 21 votes for Lindbergh out of about 350. In Emmons, he received only 2 votes! Still, there were pockets of NPL support in the county. Lindbergh carried London, Mansfield, and Pickerel Lake townships.

The editor of thc *Blooming Prairie Times* registered his disap-

The NPL had a low opinion of politicians.
The Nonpartisan Leader, March 11th, 1918.

proval of the pro-Lindbergh vote in Sibley County in a mean-spirited comment. Writing in the July 25th, 1918, edition, he said:

> Sibley County went heavily for Lindbergh and the strongest Lindbergh precincts were Bismarck and Moltke. They lived up to their names Bismarck giving Burnquist only 7 votes and Lindbergh 120 while Moltke excelled in frightfulness by giving Burnquist only one vote and Lindbergh 138.

Sibley County was heavily populated by German immigrants. Bismarck and Moltke were nineteenth century German heroes, thus, the names of the townships. To imply that a vote for Lindbergh, a former Republican Congressman of Swedish origin, was pro-German, was a low blow, but such was the situation in wartime Minnesota.

The NPL was, in the words of historian Robert L. Morlan, a "Political Prairie Fire." The group had its greatest success in the prairie counties of western Minnesota. The NPL appeal did not resonate as much in areas with diversified agriculture. Still, Mower County had the distinction of having a local candidate on the statewide ballot. Ralph E. Crane, a Grand Meadow area farmer and businessman, was on the Republican ballot as a candidate for Lieutenant-Governor, challenging incumbent Frankson. Crane was the Nonpartisan League candidate, Charles August Lindbergh's running mate. The April 1st, 1918 issue of the *The Nonpartisan Leader* had this to say about Crane:

> For lieutenant governor, the farmers chose a tried and true friend, who has served the producers of Mower County in the state legislature? He is Representative R.E. Crane."
>
> Crane was well-known. He was so well thought of by the Nonpartisan league members of his own county that, prior to the state convention of the League, he was endorsed by the League county convention for the state senate. The fact that the state convention has drafted him as a candidate for lieutenant governor makes it necessary for the Mower County League convention to reassemble and indorse [sic] another man for the state senate.

During the war, the NPL was a source of endless controversy across Minnesota. League members were sharply criticized in editorials and by their neighbors. In some cases, they were even physically attacked. What was it about the NPL that caused such acrimony? The answer requires some background.

Crane was known throughout the area. Born in Canton, New York, and a graduate of St. Lawrence University, he moved to Minnesota in 1879. He was a teacher, then principal at the Lansing school in the early 1880s, then at the Moscow school in Freeborn County. Later, he settled in the Grand Meadow area where he was a successful farmer, banker, and politician. In 1918, he was the District 5 member of the Minnesota House, representing Mower County. His association with Lindbergh and the NPL put him in the middle of an extremely controversial campaign. Crane did not have to travel far to face the wrath of people angry with the NPL.

It is impossible to make sense of all the shifting political sands in 1917-1918. In a lengthy letter to the editor in the *Austin Weekly Herald,* prominent Dexter area farmer John M. Christgau (the same John Christgau who had attacked the Herald for its supposed pro-war stance 4 months earlier) attacked Crane and the NPL "on the false principles which the league stands on . . . " Essentially, the argument was about the NPL's insistence that farmers receive a fair price for their goods from millers, packers, and banks, and in the marketplace. Christgau and anti-NPLers responded this way. "The cry of the league is, we want more money for what we produce, we are not getting our share." To Christgau and many others, concern for money had to give way to "a coordination of purposes. Of putting aside our own ambitions and desires even if sacrificing financial advantages." Anything less was selfish, disloyal, behavior.

In 1918, virtually every issue of the local newspapers carried at least one negative story or editorial comment about the NPL. They made no effort to investigate or honestly report on the legitimacy of the NPL agenda. The NPL case against the all-powerful state government, and its abuse of basic Constitutional rights was ignored. The papers published little or nothing about the behavior of the NPL's big business adversaries. The heavy-handed grain millers and other big businesses in Minneapolis were in control. Their influence with Governor Burnquist, the Commission, and the Minnesota Legislature proved to be too strong for the NPL to break.

Today it seems odd that the press would so cavalierly dismiss the First Amendment rights of anyone. The First Amendment is the core of American democracy and more than any institution, newspapers should recognize that. Yet dismiss it they did.

The Crane/Christgau feud is a prime example of the fear, anger, and hysteria that was common in 1917-1918. Christgau's attack was unfounded. The NPL was not the extreme organization he made it out to be, and Crane was not conducting "damnable politics" as a candidate for Lieutenant Governor. In fact, Crane was a good example of a patriot; he had served his community most of his adult life. For that matter, Christgau was a patriot too. Both men contributed much to the growth and prosperity of the area.

One final, ironic twist remains. Crane and Christgau each had two sons serving in the war, and Crane's younger son Wade registered for the draft in June 1918 but was not drafted. Each had a son who fought at the Meuse-Argonne, both young Mower County men served with distinction. Rollin Crane was taken prisoner on October 14th, 1918, his 26th birthday. He nearly died of starvation as he was moved through 4 German POW camps. At war's end he was hospitalized for months, suffering from a hernia and diphtheria, as well as the effects of starvation. One wonders what their fathers thought of the angry words when the war was over.

10

VOLUNTEERS

A Message from T.R.

The most important task before us is to get the largest possible number of effective troops at the front at the earliest possible moment. Second only in importance to this is the further work of the Red Cross in providing for more of these troops and in giving aid to our hard pressed and war-torn allies.

The Red Cross is doing this in a masterly fashion under a great and efficient organization. I most earnestly bespeak the fullest support for it from every man and woman in the United States. Let each give the utmost amount possible according to his or her ability. Let every man serve with his body if possible and if this is not possible, at least let him do everything with his purse to help the soldiers at the front and all who suffer bodily ill because of the war.

—Theodore Roosevelt,
Owatonna Journal-Chronicle, June 22nd, 1917

Workers Needed

> Do not forget the work at the Red Cross rooms. Much work is needed in the surgical dressing department and more than 100 pneumonia jackets are still needed for the shipment which must be made by November 1.

–*Mower County Transcript-Republican,*
October 23rd, 1918

Across the country, millions of Americans volunteered their time and money to support the war effort. Southern Minnesota was no exception. The variety of groups that were organized, and the causes they represented, is astonishing. Most people wanted to own a piece of the war, to support the effort in any way they could. Almost everyone had a friend or relative who was in the fight, but even those who did not felt an impulse to help. When looking at the lists of volunteers, the work that they did, and the money they raised, it is clear that people really did make great sacrifices.

In Mower County, at least 15 separate organizations actively raised money and called upon the time and talents of residents for support. Steele and Freeborn Counties had similar experiences. Thousands of people volunteered.

By far, the largest volunteer effort involved the Red Cross. Local membership in the Red Cross and all its auxiliaries was remarkable. In December 1917, Freeborn County reported a total membership of 6,249 people, about one quarter of the county's population.

Almost from the moment war was declared, women and men across southern Minnesota volunteered. Women knit socks and sweaters, sewed hospital garments, and made surgical dressings and helmets. School children were organized and did what they could for the war effort.

First up to organize a Red Cross branch in Mower County, was the Ladies Floral Club. The club, the oldest women's club in Minnesota, (it is still going strong today) had been around for almost of the time the city of Austin had been in existence. In May 1917, the club endorsed the idea of a Red Cross branch in Mower County and appointed a committee to work with other Mower County organizations toward that goal. Shortly thereafter, the Art and Travel club joined in the effort. The clubs, led by the wives of prominent Austin citizens, solicited a list of charter members for the Austin chapter. Many of the names are still familiar today. Hormel, Banfield, Catherwood, Nicolson, West, Hogan, Wold, and Avery all played important roles in organizing the Red Cross. No doubt the support of such illustrious citizens helped make the organization a success.

By June 1917, the organization was on its way. Bylaws were adopted, and a board of directors elected. Once again, the board was composed of community leaders both male and female. The organization had two purposes. The first was raising money. In that effort, they were successful. Leaders, aware of its popularity, associated themselves with Chautauqua. When large numbers of people gathered in Lafayette Park for the Austin Chautauqua programs in June, local Red Cross volunteers were there to solicit funds. Reports say that the fund drive raised $17,000, a remarkable sum of money for an organization that had only existed for about two months. $10,000 of the total was sent to national Red Cross headquarters; the balance, $7,000 remained as working money for local Red Cross efforts.[138]

Red Cross headquarters were established in a building on East Water Street. Various work units were created within the city

138. Nicholsen, Mower County in the World War, 216.

of Austin, and the entire county was organized throughout the summer and fall of 1917. Branches and auxiliaries from 16 Mower County communities were represented on the board of directors. By November, the name had been changed to the Mower County Chapter. From then until the signing of the armistice, hundreds of men and women volunteered in any way they could to support Red Cross projects.

The official Mower County history, Mower County in the Great War compiled by John and Gertrude Skinner, has extensive lists of useful items created and money raised by County residents for the Red Cross. Garments of all kinds, socks, shirts, pinafores, shawls, sweaters, and mufflers were handcrafted and sent to American troops and European refugees. Surgical dressings were also made and shipped by the Mower County chapter.

In Freeborn County, the women's auxiliary created comfort kits for every county man entering the service. Working out of the Wedge-Jones building in Albert Lea, seamstresses made a total of 1,014 kit bags in 1918.

Red Cross volunteers kept meticulous records. In August 1919, local Red Cross president C.F. Cook was complimented by a Northern Division auditor who said that the Mower County records were "the most perfect of any he had examined in the entire district." Everything was accounted for, including the names of volunteers and the number of hours they worked. At the end of the war, 71 Mower County women were honored for working more than 800 hours each in the Hospital Garments department. In total, volunteers made articles with an estimated value in excess of $52,000. Additionally, Mower County residents donated over $102,000 to the Red Cross from June 1917 until June 1919.

Similarly extensive records were kept in Owatonna. The January 1918 sewing and knitting report is a story of dedication and sacrifice on the homefront that was common in 1917-18. The report shows that 997 people worked a total of 2,384 hours in the Red Cross sewing rooms. Volunteer time was credited in 5-minute increments. For example, 16 Pythian Sisters worked a total of 39 hours and 10 minutes. Furthermore, many Steele County volunteers worked from their homes, cutting and sewing. Again, their names and the number and type of articles they produced was dutifully reported.

In August of 1917, a reporter at the *Owatonna Journal-Chronicle* had some fun with a request for sewing volunteers. The headline read "Seamstresses Seek Sewing Susies To Sew Sammies' Sox." Not only that, but the request was made by Stella Smith! The idea was to get young women, presumably students on summer vacation, to come to the high school in Owatonna for sewing sessions.

The Red Cross also played a vital role in civilian relief. Communication with the War Department was important. Parents who had not heard from their sons for some time often found that the Red Cross could trace them. Anxious parents or wives who had not received their much-needed financial allotments were sometimes given temporary assistance until funds arrived. The organization also played a vital role in helping the families of soldiers who were wounded or who had perished in battle or in the influenza epidemic.

Local chapters of the Red Cross were also quick to respond to emergencies closer to home. The Freeborn County chapter raised in excess of $4,400 for victims of the devastating forest fires that swept across northern Minnesota in the autumn of 1918. The fires, one of the worst natural disasters in Minnesota history, killed over 450 people and laid waste to many thousands of acres. The Cloquet-Moose Lake area was hit especially hard. Hayward Township farmers sent a carload of hay and straw to the Red Cross chapter there for distribution to farmers in the burned-out area.[139]

The fires were a tragic Minnesota story during the war, and the Red Cross was not alone in working to aid victims. Statewide, overall responsibility for assisting the area was in the hands of the Public Safety Commission. It acted as an umbrella organization in charge of relief efforts across the state. The Commission delegated responsibility to local groups that did the actual work. Within days, foodstuffs and money were already coming into local organizations. In Steele County, newspapers published lists of donors, even for amounts as small as $1. Residents responded generously and quickly. In Mower County, the Village of Adams was the first to raise its quota established by the Commission. Overall, in Mower County, about $8,000 was raised for fire relief, along with clothing and vegetables which were sent to victims.[140]

In an interesting twist on fundraising, Freeborn County dairymen developed a unique way of helping the Red Cross. By late 1917, travelers on Freeborn County roads often encountered a sign proclaiming, "We milk cows for the American Red Cross." Based on an idea from John D. Ruble, a patron of Albert Lea State Creamery, producers were encouraged to pledge a percentage of their milk check to the Red Cross. A committee was established, with representatives from each creamery responsible for explaining the program to patrons. From the beginning, it was clear that every farmer was expected to pledge. The committees refused to take no for an answer, even if it took a second visit from more assertive solicitors. Nine Freeborn County creameries participated in the program, deducting the farmer's contribution from his milk check and forwarding it to the Red Cross. In all, 546 farmers subscribed.[141]

139. Wood, *In the World War: Freeborn County.*

140. Nicholsen, *Mower County in the World War,* 216.

141. Wood, *In the World War: Freeborn County.*

There were many other causes to which people donated, and volunteered their time. The YMCA conducted two major fund drives. The YMCA was essential to the war effort. The organization worked closely with the United States Army, providing services for soldiers far from home. In the first fund drive, in May 1917, Austin and Mower County raised over $1,000. In November of 1917, the YMCA conducted a second fund. In this case, the quota was $14,000. Attorney F. G. Sasse of Austin was in charge and the county vastly exceeded its quota, raising $23,000. Mower County was the first county in the state to raise its quota.

Successful fundraisers were ruthless and willing to use any advantage they had. One such man was Father Gmeinder of St. Peter's in Rose Creek, a YMCA solicitor. The good Father, spotting a barrel of beer at the railroad depot addressed to a man who refused to donate, ordered that the beer not be delivered until the recipient came across with the money. "He collected a good donation from the consignee before the wet goods were delivered. Father Gmeinder did splendid work all the drives." Father Gmeinder must have been a dynamic individual. He was a star in local fundraising circles. At a large gathering in November 1917, sponsored by the Knights of Columbus, Austin attorney Sasse commended him for his help in the YMCA cause. To some extent, doctrinal differences were set aside during the war. Sasse even urged Protestants to help the Knights of Columbus in their work.[142]

In a rare case of under- subscription, at least in Mower County, the Salvation Army failed to reach its fundraising goal of $15,000. Mower County raised just $4,000. Other, more successful campaigns included Belgium Relief, Clothing for Needy Europe, the Near East Drive (the only drive run by women), and the United War Work Campaign.

142. Nicholsen, *Mower County in the World War*, 219.

In Minnesota, rotary clubs and the America First Association raised funds for an entertainment ticketing scheme for service members. The "Smileage" books were little booklets each containing 20 coupons, each coupon good for admittance to a program of entertainment.

Mower County also participated in the Jewish Relief Fund, not a cause that immediately comes to mind in southern Minnesota. Austin Mayor George Hirsch was chairman of the local drive, and contributions were sought through columns in the *Austin Daily Herald*, not through active solicitation. Even without solicitors, in a free will offering, Mower County oversubscribed its allotment of $500 in just two weeks. On August 5th, 1918, shortly after the American Jewish Relief Committee for Sufferers from the War received the Mower County funds, national chairman Henry Morgenthau responded with a thank you letter addressed to the *Herald*. The letter goes to the core of what it means to be an American. Morgenthau wrote, "The generosity of American Citizenship without regard to creed or color in this campaign has touched me deeply. It expresses in no uncertain terms the solidarity of our people in the cause of humanity and democracy for which our brave boys are so heroically struggling in the trenches of France."[143]

During all the wartime turmoil, one fund drive stands out for having a bit of unintended humor. The Tobacco Fund was supposed to be used for the purchase American tobacco for our boys "over there." Apparently, American troops had a hard time getting used to the tobacco used by their British and French compatriots. As a result, the "Boys in France Tobacco Fund" was set up, the idea being to provide the troops with the American "weed" they preferred. Naturally, some busybodies, acting as morality police, made their

143. Ibid., 220.

displeasure with the drive's purpose known in letters to the editor. Other, worldlier citizens supported the Fund with their funds. Contribution boxes were strategically placed in pool halls, tobacco stores, and hotel and club rooms. In an ironic twist, the money raised at William's Cigar Store in downtown Austin was stolen by thieves who broke in through the establishment's rear window. They escaped with a grand total of $5.75. Smoking must have been popular in southern Minnesota. At the end of the war it was reported that the city of Austin ranked 17th nationally for the amount contributed to the tobacco fund.[144]

Religious institutions were an important part of the lives of many in southern Minnesotan. Church membership was high, much higher than it is a century later. Churches, and church affiliated organizations such as the Knights of Columbus were critically important during the war. Father Gmeinder of Rose Creek has already been mentioned, using his moral authority to raise money for the YMCA. Fundraising was important, but it was only a part of the role played by churches and the clergy.

Freeborn County clergymen, led by Reverend L.W. Stekel, created a "Pulpit Publicity Committee." The committee, an ecumenical organization, recognized that they had a large constituency listening to them every week. Essentially, they used their influence to promote wartime activities. They were called upon for sermons on war aims, and they coordinated announcements about fund drives and other activities.

Clergymen used the power of the pulpit, not only to teach the message of the gospel and raise wartime morale, but also to guide their parishioners "along the right lines." In other words, sermons and other church functions were used to support American war aims and foster patriotism.

144. Ibid., 222.

"A great net of mercy drawn through an ocean of unspeakable pain"

The Greatest Mother in the World

STRETCHING forth her hands to all in need; to Jew or Gentile, black or white; knowing no favorite, yet favoring all.

Ready and eager to comfort at a time when comfort is most needed. Helping the little home that's crushed beneath an iron hand, by showing mercy in a healthy, human way; re-building it, in fact, with stone on stone; replenishing empty bins and empty cupboards; bringing warmth to hearts and hearths too long neglected.

Seeing all things with a mother's seventh sense that's blind to jealousy and meanness; seeing men in their true light as naughty children—snatching, biting, bitter—but with a hidden side that's quickest touched by mercy.

Reaching out her hands across the sea to No Man's Land to cheer with warmer comforts thousands who must stand and wait in stenched and crawling holes and watersoaked entrenchments where cold and wet bite deeper, so they write, than Boche steel or lead.

She's warming thousands, feeding thousands, healing thousands from her store; the Greatest Mother in the World—the Red Cross.

Your help is needed—give till the heart says stop.

Every cent of every dollar received for the Red Cross War Fund goes for War Relief.

The American Red Cross is the largest and most efficient organization for the relief of suffering that the World has ever seen.

It is made up almost entirely of volunteer workers, the higher executives being without exception men accustomed to large affairs, who are in almost all cases giving their services without pay.

It is supported entirely by its membership fees and by voluntary contributions.

It is today bringing relief to suffering humanity, both military and civil, in every War torn allied country.

It plans tomorrow to help in the work of restoration throughout the world.

It feeds and clothes entire populations in times of great calamity.

It is there to help your soldier boy in his time o need.

With its thousands of workers, its tremendous stores and smooth running transportation facilities it is serving as America's advance guard—and thu helping to win the war.

Congress authorizes it.

President Wilson heads it.

The War Department audits its accounts.

Your Army, your Navy and your Allies enthusiastically endorse it.

Twenty-two million Americans have joined it.

THIS SPACE DONATED BY BLOOMING PRAIRIE CRY. ASSO.

Red Cross ads were designed to appeal on an emotional level.

Blooming Prairie Times, May 16th, 1918.

> It can be recorded that the trumpet of the church sounded no uncertain note when this nation was preparing for battle. The clergymen answered every call for speakers to advocate for the cause of loyalty. They went out in all kinds of weather by train to far distant points of the state or by auto to various parts of the county.[145]

It was not the first, and certainly not the last time, that politics and religion have mixed in American life. However, it is a bit jarring to consider that a minister in Germany, and a minister in Owatonna, or Albert Lea, perhaps even members of the same denomination, would each be praying for victory on Sunday morning, both assuring their flocks that "God is with us."

Local histories, and newspapers, contain the names of thousands of citizens who volunteered in some capacity. The war was for everyone, not just men and women in uniform, and volunteers were essential. Their generous contribution helped make victory possible.

145. Ibid., 252.

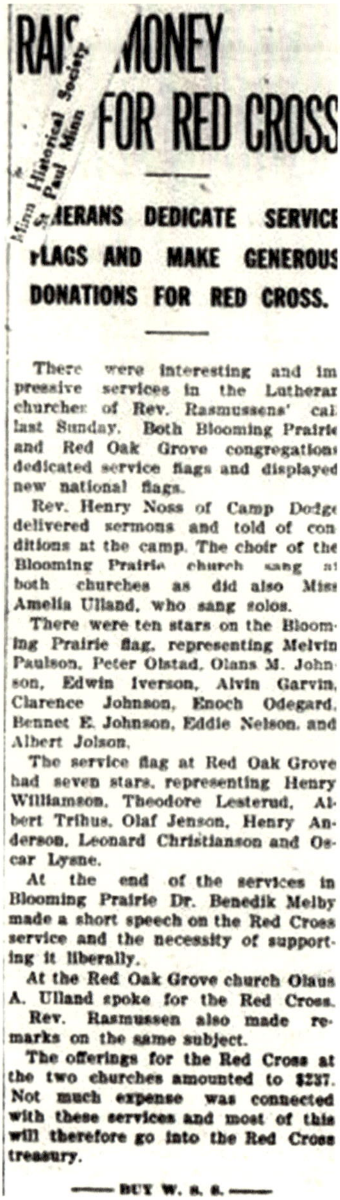

RAISE MONEY FOR RED CROSS

LUTHERANS DEDICATE SERVICE FLAGS AND MAKE GENEROUS DONATIONS FOR RED CROSS.

There were interesting and impressive services in the Lutheran churches of Rev. Rasmussens' call last Sunday. Both Blooming Prairie and Red Oak Grove congregations dedicated service flags and displayed new national flags.

Rev. Henry Noss of Camp Dodge delivered sermons and told of conditions at the camp. The choir of the Blooming Prairie church sang at both churches as did also Miss Amelia Ulland, who sang solos.

There were ten stars on the Blooming Prairie flag, representing Melvin Paulson, Peter Olstad, Olans M. Johnson, Edwin Iverson, Alvin Garvin, Clarence Johnson, Enoch Odegard, Bennet E. Johnson, Eddie Nelson, and Albert Jolson.

The service flag at Red Oak Grove had seven stars, representing Henry Williamson, Theodore Lesterud, Albert Trihus, Olaf Jenson, Henry Anderson, Leonard Christianson and Oscar Lysne.

At the end of the services in Blooming Prairie Dr. Benedik Melby made a short speech on the Red Cross service and the necessity of supporting it liberally.

At the Red Oak Grove church Olaus A. Ulland spoke for the Red Cross.

Rev. Rasmussen also made remarks on the same subject.

The offerings for the Red Cross at the two churches amounted to $237. Not much expense was connected with these services and most of this will therefore go into the Red Cross treasury.

—— BUY W. S. S. ——

Churches were heavily involved in the war effort.

Blooming Prairie Times, April 11th, 1918.

11

FARMERS AND WOMEN FEED AMERICA AND THE WORLD

"Food will win the war." –Herbert Hoover

"The allies need more wheat, more meat, more sugar. It is either wheatless and meatless days for us or wheatless and meatless months for them."[146]

"Of all the important foods, wheat bread contains the most nutrition. Bread made from Pillsbury's Best Flour is richer in nourishment than any other food article that the world has produced."[147]

"How much did you increase the crop of 1917? How much more can you add to the 1918 crop with the time now left?"[148]

---

146. Committee on Public Information: Four Minute Men Division. *Sample Speech.*
147. The Pillsbury Flour Mills Co. *The Pillsbury Cookbook,* 10.
148. J. F. Fleming et al., *The Cooperative Manager and Farmer,* 7, no.1 (September 1917) 1.

The war was always in people's thoughts, but, as always, countless daily tasks had to be completed. Hard work was made even harder due to the loss of many young men serving in the military. On the home front, farmers and food processors were on the front lines. With their specialized knowledge, land, and livestock, they had an essential role in wartime America. Farmers supplied more than food and fiber; many horses were needed in France, and scrap iron from worn out machinery was in demand as well.

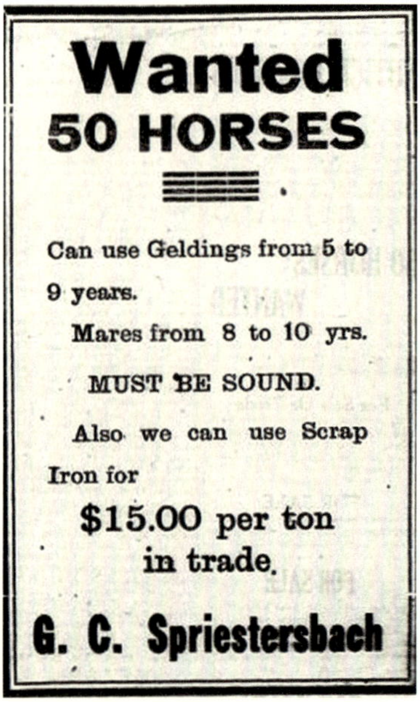

Horses and iron needed in wartime.
Blooming Prairie Times, July 5th, 1917.

It's no exaggeration to say that American farmers fed the world. Their ability to produce was critical to many people across the globe; not just to soldiers, but to children and families in war-torn Europe. The daily ration for draftees in the training camps was 4,000 calories; soldiers need a lot of food. Their requirements were nearly double that of citizens on the homefront who observed the suggested wartime restrictions.[149] Conservation and sacrifice were necessary if everyone was to be fed, and government agencies, both federal and state, played active roles in the process.

149. Rae Katherine Eighmey, *Food Will Win the War: Minnesota Crops, Cooks, and Conservation During World War I*, 8.

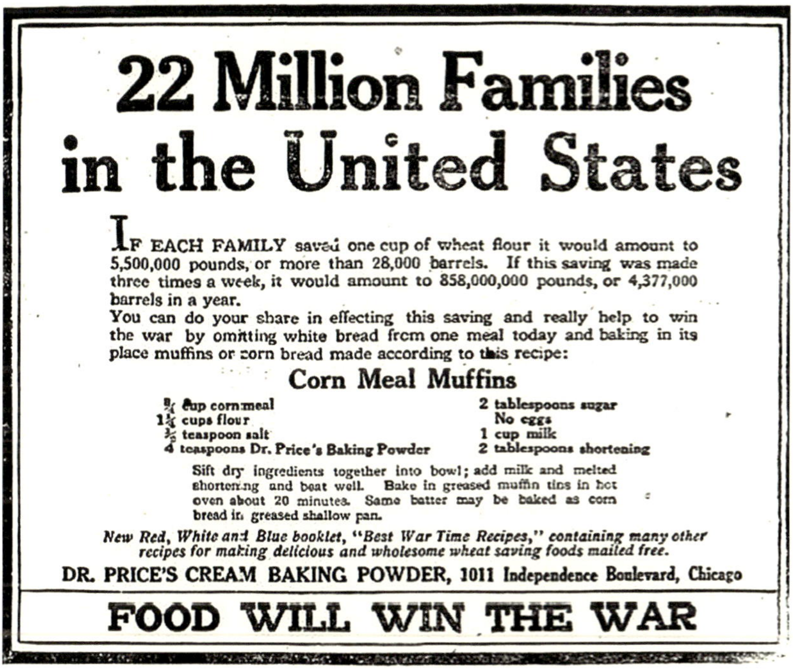

The government tried to limit the domestic consumption of wheat.
Freeborn County Standard, March 7th, 1918.

In addition, American allies in Europe, both troops and civilians, needed other sources of food because of the chaos on the battlefields and the disruption of traditional trading patterns. Herbert Hoover, a wealthy, Iowa-born mining engineer, emerged as an international leader in the effort to feed innocent victims of the war. He became chairman of the Committee for the Relief of Belgium and proved to be particularly adroit at raising money for food and convincing the warring powers to allow food shipments into occupied Belgium. From 1914-1917, his organizational talents helped save the lives of many Belgians. Recognizing his ability, Woodrow Wilson appointed him to head the U.S. Food Administration soon after the U.S. entered the conflict.

Congress created the U.S. Food Administration (USFA) in August 1917 to further U.S. security interests by encouraging food production and conservation. The USFA emphasized food conservation, and preservation through educational campaigns. "Hooverize" became a synonym for avoiding food waste. They also instituted price controls and some rationing of basic food products. Farm production was also stimulated.[150] In practice, this meant that Minnesota consumers and farmers had both federal and state government agencies advising them.

With the advent of war, surpluses vanished. Many products were in short supply, so the ability of Minnesota farmers to produce was critical. Minnesota was one of the top states in the nation in the production of butter, grains, and meat. The state was also home to large flour milling and meatpacking industries. Good

150. Raymond Pearl, and Magdalen H. Burger. "Retail Prices of Food During 1917 and 1918." *Publications of the American Statistical Association*, 16, no. 127 (1919): 411-39. Accessed November 2nd, 2020. doi:10.2307/2964812.

The U.S Food Administration distributed many propaganda posters.
Paul Stahr, 1918. Library of Congress Prints and Photographs Division Washington, D.C.

farmers and productive land meant that southern Minnesota was a key to the state's overall production.

There was a difference in perspective between farm and city residents. The high prices farmers received for their livestock and crops meant high prices in the grocery store. Naturally, that presented a challenge for urban women trying to feed their families. The March 6th, 1918, edition of the *Austin Weekly Herald* contains a letter reprinted from *The Farmer* magazine. The letter's author, a Minnesota farm wife, admonished her city counterparts, urging them to remember all the expense and work required before food items appeared in the grocery store. She went into detail about the tough conditions on the farm. She wanted city dwellers to think before they complained about the price of food.

"One of the fundamental purposes of the Food Administration was to do everything possible to regulate and keep the retail prices of staple articles of food at a minimum to the consumer."[151] They did so with the help of reliable volunteers who visited representative grocery stores each week and reported on a list of 28 food staples. They filed their reports on printed forms which were turned in, and then released to the newspapers. They were published on a regular basis. It was not price control as such, but the reports did make food prices more transparent for consumers. It was another example of the government's effort to ensure that everyone was treated fairly.

Mechanization was beginning to transform American agriculture, and it was one way to get around the shortage of help, but farming was still a labor-intensive business. The cows had to be milked twice a day, usually by hand. The cream was separated and delivered to the local creamery. Animals were fed, barns cleaned, manure hauled to the field, and eggs picked, every day, including Sundays and holidays. In their season, crops had to be planted

151. Ibid.

FAIR FOOD PRICES

PREPARED UNDER DIRECTION OF THE UNITED STATES FOOD ADMINISTRATION.

Sugar, Granulated	8.08	.09½ to .10

Not over 5 lbs. to a customer in city or 10 lbs. to a customer in the country. Name of purchaser and amount of each purchase must be kept by dealer making such sale.

Sugar, Cut Loaf		9.75	.12½ to	.15
Sugar, Brown	7.75	to 8.25	.09½ to	.10
Flour, 24½ lbs.	1.38	to 1.42	1.55	to 1.60

Not over 24½ lbs. to a customer in city or 49 lbs. to a customer in the country, and in any case not to exceed 30 days' supply, estimated upon the basis of 6 lbs. per month to each person in the family. Dealers to sell wheat flour only with an equal weight of other cereal flours or meals. Consumers have choice of corn meal, corn starch, corn flour, hominy, corn grits, barley flour, rice, rice flour, oatmeal, rolled oats, buckwheat flour. Rye flour is not considered a substitute for wheat flour.

	Wholesale			**Retail Range**		
Barley Flour, 10 lb. sack............	.77½	to	.80	.90	to	.95
Rye Flour, 10 lb. sack..............	.70	to	.75	.80	to	.85
Buckwheat Flour, 10 lb. sack........	.80	to	.85	.95	to	1.00
Graham, 10 lb. sack................	.50	to	.55	.65	to	.70
Whole Wheat, 10 lb. sack............	.50	to	.55	.65	to	.70
Corn Flour, Bulk, per lb............	.06	to	.07	.08	to	.09
Corn Meal, 10 lb. sack..............	.55	to	.60	.70	to	.75
Evap. Milk, Tall Cans, each.........	.12	to	.12½	.14	to	.15
Evap. Milk, Small Cans, each........	.05½	to	.06	.07	to	.08
Beans, per lb......................	.13¾	to	.14	.17	to	.18
Soy Beans	.07	to	.08	.09	to	.10
Syrup, Corn, 5 lb. cans.............	.34	to	.37½	.45	to	.50
Syrup, 10 lb. cans..................	.64	to	.75	.85	to	.90
Potatoes, per cwt...................	.90	to	1.00	1.00	to	1.10
New Cabbage, per lb.................	.05	to	.06	.07	to	.08
Butter, per lb., Creamery...........	.44	to	.45	.48	to	.49
Eggs, per doz.	.30			.34	to	.35
Oleomargarine	.25	to	.31	.30	to	.35
Cheese, Twins	.21	to	.25½	.32	to	.35
Cheese, Brick			.22	.28	to	.35
Bacon Strips, fancy.................	.40	to	.42	.45	to	.50
Bacon Strips, sugar cured...........	.36	to	.38	.41	to	.43
Hams, Best, Whole...................	.31	to	.33	.33	to	.35
Hams, Sugar Cured, Whole............	.30	to	.32	.33	to	.34
Hams, Picnic, Whole.................	.21	to	.23	.25	to	.27
Lard, Best	.27½	to	.28	.32	to	.35
Lard Substitute Compound............	.23	to	.25	.28	to	.30
Pickerel	.12	to	.13	.13	to	.16
Halibut	.23			.28	to	.30
Salmon	.23	to	.30	.28	to	.35
Rolled Oats, 55 oz. Pkg.............	.24	to	.27	.30	to	.35
Rice, Fancy Head....................	.10	to	.11	.13	to	.15
Rice, Broken	.07	to	.08	.10	to	.11

Lists like this appeared in local newspapers.
Freeborn County Standard, June 24th, 1918.

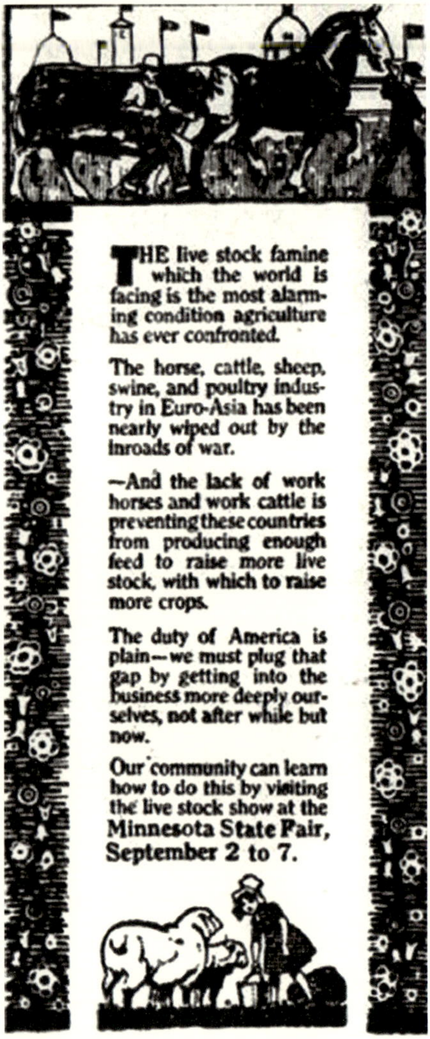

Minnesotan farmers took their duty to produce seriously.
Blooming Prairie Times, July 25th, 1918.

and harvested. The work never stopped.

Prices were at record levels for most farm products. Demand had never been higher. Prices were easy to track, as most newspapers updated market quotes in every edition. Wheat that sold for $0.85 per bushel in 1914 was well over $2.00 in 1918. Hog prices had doubled to around $0.16 per pound. Turkeys were at $0.25 per pound. Cattle prices were higher too, and dairymen were getting record prices for butterfat. In Corning, the Red Oak Grove Creamery was paying $0.67 per pound in October 1918 compared to $0.30 in 1914.

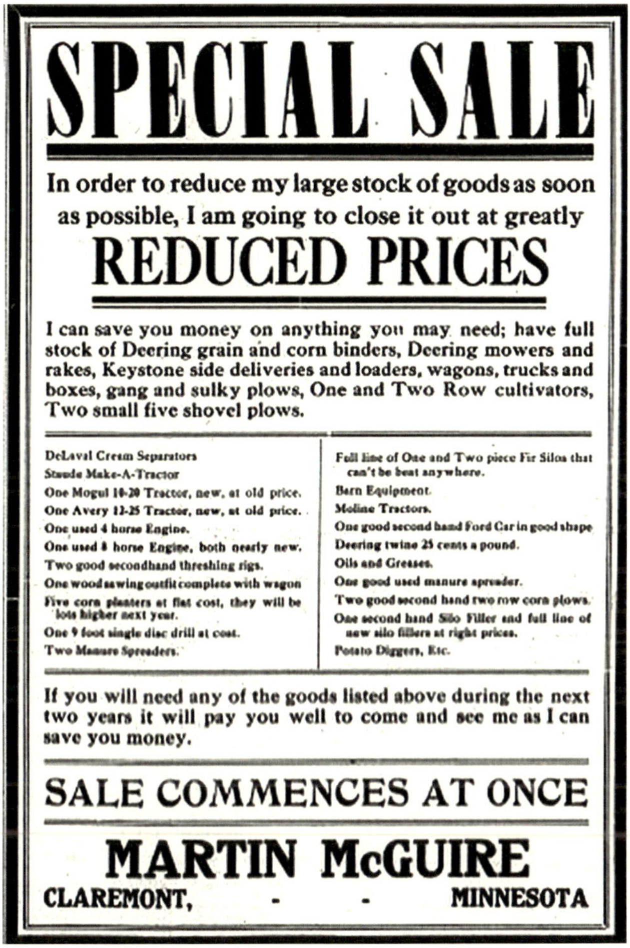

One solution to the labor shortage was modern machinery. Gasoline tractors were just coming on the scene.
People's Press, June 14th, 1918.

A "Delco" system to generate electricity made milking machines and other electric devices possible. Ads like these were common in area newspapers in 1918.
Freeborn County Standard, March 11th, 1918.

ILOS ON OUR FARMS HELP THE SOLDIERS ON THE FIRING LINES

The federal food administration is calling on the farmers of Minnesota to build silos, and to build them now. The food administration is making the same appeal to the farmers of other states. The reason for the call is that the silo increases the prosperity of the farm and thereby strengthens the organization on which the nation and its associate nations in the war depend

What Makes a Good Silo.

Air-tight walls.
Smooth walls (inside).
Water-proof walls.
Strength to resist winds.
Durability.
Round walls, to facilitate filling and packing.
Attractiveness.

Location of the Silo.

Both the Federal and State government promoted the use of silos to preserve fodder and enhance farm prosperity. Dairy farmers used them extensively.
Freeborn County Standard, June 17th, 1918.

Financially, it was a good time to be a farmer, but good help was hard to find. As one would expect in Minnesota, the Commission was ready to help. In fact, efficient food production was part of their responsibility. In 1917, local County Commission branches were given responsibility for setting up labor bureaus to recruit and organize help for hard pressed farmers. It was not clear just how helpful untrained people could be in the demanding work on the farm. However the bureaus were created, and the 1917 and 1918 harvests were gathered.

There is a bit of unintended humor in the accounts of the Steele County Commission organizational meeting as reported in the July 1st, 1917, issue of *The Daily People's Press*. Blooming Prairie Banker and State Senator, Sam Rask, along with other "city people" at the meeting were anxious to aid farmers who found themselves short of labor due to the draft. Rask declared:

> Men are needed behind the lines to husband the crops if we have one. In Blooming Prairie, we have organized to do this and all businessmen, if necessary, will close their business to assist. It is not a charitable proposition. We have agreed to go out and do what we can and to accept payment for what we are worth.

Steele County farmers, perhaps wise in the ways of their city brethren, were cautious about the offer of help.

George Bush, a local farmer at the meeting, was sceptical of Rask's idea. *The People's Press* reported on his comments: "George Bush urged caution on the labor problem, declaring that a farmer could not use city men, unfamiliar with farm work, because the green hands could not be of any real assistance and could not earn real wages." In other words, "city slickers" need not apply. It must have been an aggravating situation for many farmers; the Commission, as always, seemed to have good advice about how they should proceed. Sometimes one can receive too much free advice, and the Commission seemed to have an answer, though not the wisdom, for everything. From labor to grain grading, and even building silos, they were not shy about lecturing farmers.

It is interesting to note that the Commission took the farm labor shortage so seriously, that in March of 1918 they suggested that the federal government release newly conscripted farmers to help at critical times on the farm. How that could be accomplished during their military training was never explained.

In July of 1918, the Commission adopted a statement designed to draw attention to the labor problem. The announcement declared the 1918 Minnesota hay and small grain crop to be, in their words, "phenomenal." Harvest help was needed. They even invoked the Bible in their quest to get every able-bodied person, even idlers, out of cities and towns and into the fields to help, by saying: "There is a cry from the farmers in the country as loud as the cry from Macedonia in Bible times." The Commission urged that other work be postponed if possible, because of the urgent need for harvest help.[152]

Threshermen were required by law to register their machines, and eventually county agents working in conjunction with the Farm Bureau and the owners of large threshing machines instituted procedures and prices for the 1918 harvest. Wages were set by the threshing foreman. The steam engines required skilled operators who could earn five to six dollars per day—twice that of a laborer pitching bundles. The price of threshing was set too. Typically,

---

152. Burnquist et. al., *Report of Minnesota Commission of Public Safety*, 147-148.

FARM HELP WANTED

The Farm Labor Problem is serious, but it can be solved. There is a movement to mobilize town men of farm experience for a few days at a time or for certain days of the week during the periods of labor strain in haying and harvest. This was done here successfully to some extent last year. It is not the best labor; the town men are not "hard," but they can at least work a few hours a day and in the aggregate they can furnish the necessary man-power for emergencies.

If you are willing to enlist to help Save the Crop in this community fill out the following form and either mail or bring the same to Sam A. Rask, Local Labor Agent.

Blooming Prairie, Minn 1918

To Sam A. Rask, Local Labor Agent,
Blooming Prairie, Minnesota.

Sir:—

The undersigned desires to be enrolled for farm work during the season of 1918.

1. Kind of work ....
2. Probable duration of work ....
3. When available ....
4. Wages wanted ....
5. Days of the week ....
6. Remarks ....

....

Signed ....

Farm Labor enrollment in the Blooming Prairie area.
Blooming Prairie Times, July 25th, 1918.

farmers paid $0.08 per bushel for wheat, and six for oats and barley. Neighbors worked together, and town people came to help. The harvest was successfully gathered.[153]

Locally and nationally, women were essential to the war effort, contributing in countless ways. Some activities like volunteering

153. Eighmey, *Food Will Win the War,* 63-64

Olaus Ulland farm Newry Township circa 1914-15: Threshing required a big crew. There are six men in this photo, with more in the field gathering bundles of grain. At least one man would have been required to tend the threshing machine and steam engine as well. It would have been hard to find a crew of that size in 1917-1918.
Dean Ulland, private collection.

for the Red Cross and Liberty Loan drives, where women were heavily involved, have already been discussed. There were other programs organized at Federal and State levels, often involving food production and preservation that were designed to be carried out locally. Frequently, these were managed by women. Food Conservation and Hoover Pledge Cards committees demonstrated methods for canning vegetables and baking bread. The Hoover cards themselves were designed to encourage everyone to conserve. Signing the card meant a commitment to conserve food. Hoover set the tone in the introduction to the *Win the War Cookbook* published in 1917.

> Go back to the simple life, be contented with simple food, simple pleasures, simple clothes. work hard, pray hard, play hard. Work, eat, recreate, and sleep. Do it all courageously. We have a victory to win.[154]

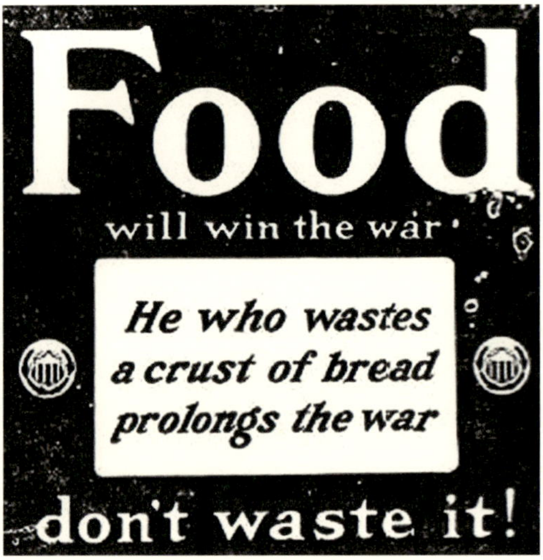

"Food will win the war"
Freeborn County Standard,
February 28th, 1918.

Women had especially difficult lives during the war. Food preparation and conservation was usually done on coal or wood burning stoves. Labor-saving devices were few, and families were

154. Reah Jennette Lynch, compiler. *Win the War Cookbook*, (St. Louis: St. Louis County unit, Woman's committee, Council of national defense, Missouri division, 1917), 8.

I ASK that every woman will fill in this blank, cut it out and send it to me.

Herbert Hoover

MR. HERBERT HOOVER, WASHINGTON, D.C.:

I am glad to join you in the service of food conservation for our nation and I hereby accept membership in the United States food administration, pledging myself to carry out the directions and advice of the food administrator in the conduct of my household, in so far as my circumstances permit.

Name____________________

Address____________________

Number of persons in family____________________

The Hoover Pledge appeared in multiple women's magazines. The Commission, University of Minnesota, and local organizations cooperated in demonstrations of conservation.

THURSDAY, FEB. 28, 1918. FREEBORN COUNTY STANDARD, ALBERT LEA, MINN. PAGE SEV

MEATLESS AND WHEATLESS DAYS

are Sure Steps Toward Fightless Days

Meatless Tuesday Wheatless Monday and Wednesday Porkless Saturday

SAVE MONEY
on YOUR GROCERIES

We introduced the cash and carry system to Albert Lea and saved our customers hundreds of dollars. We can save money for you. Come in with your list and compare prices; we want your business and can hold it if you give yourself and us a chance.

Eternal vigilance in food conservation is the price of victory in this war.

At least three times each day, every man, woman and child in this country who enjoys moderate means, has an opportunity to assist the victory.

At least three times each day people are beset with the temptation to break the food conservation rules—which means to handicap the cause and to postpone the day of victory and peace.

Appetite is a fickle thing—a thing hard to control.
The sale of Liberty bonds is accomplished when the purchaser signs on the dotted line but the food conservation idea must be sold daily and repeatedly to thousands and thousands of people.

Buy Your Meat Here

Specials for Saturday

Whitings, a fresh fish, few bones and sweet meat, try this fish. Per lb. **10c**

Salt Mackeral per lb. . . . **28c** Holland Herring per lb. . . . **15c**

Citizens were urged to go meatless and wheatless to preserve staples or the war effort.
Freeborn County Standard,
February 28th, 1918.

larger then than they are today. Rural women were called upon to help with farm work, and women in cities and towns had to stretch food budgets to feed their families. Many still found time to volunteer in church, for the Red Cross, and elsewhere.

Men and women seemed to find inner reserves of strength during the war. Tasks that needed to be done were done. Most folks adapted, working together in ways they could not have imagined before the war. Sometimes they could even enjoy a movie.

Lunchtime for the threshers at the Olaus Ulland farm, Newry Township, circa 1914-15. Farming was labor intensive business. Dean Ulland, private collection.

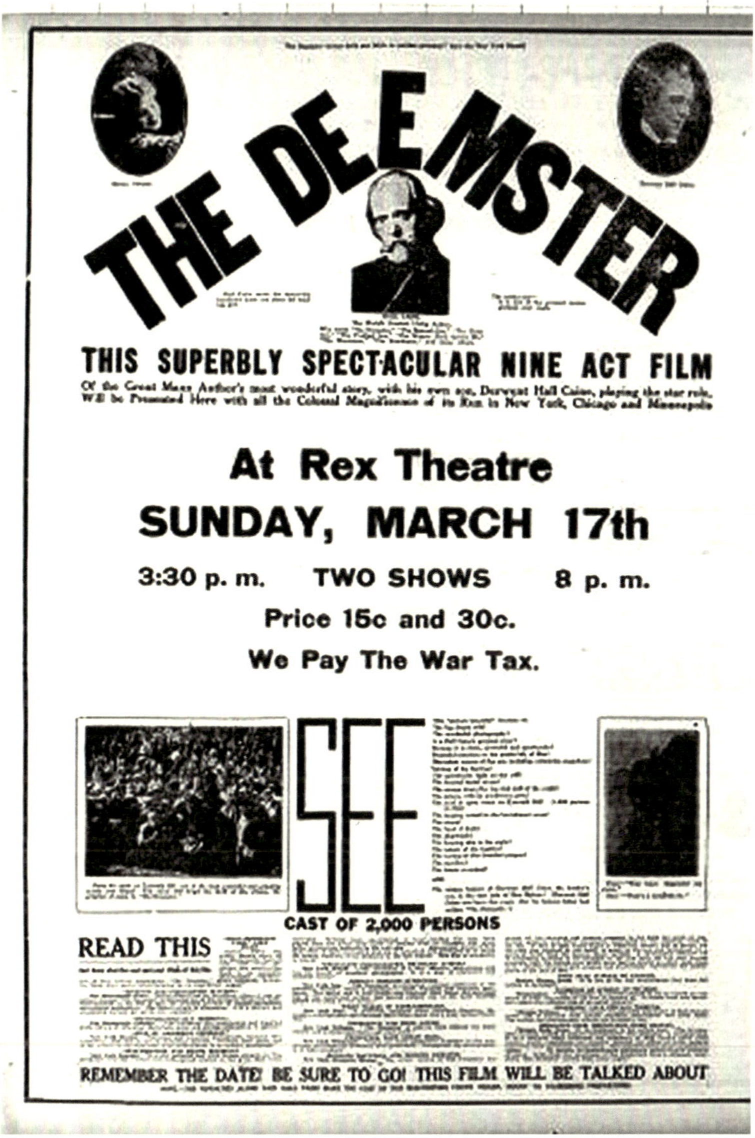

People needed entertainment,
theaters were popular.
Blooming Prairie Times, March 14th, 1918.

A Commission-produced cartoon.
Freeborn County Standard, May 6th, 1918.

FREEBORN COUNTY STANDARD, ALBERT LEA, MINN.

UNCLE SAM'S PARTNER

(Courtesy of Life and Charles Dana Gibson)

Planting home gardens, producing more food, and saving food are all war-time effort this government in which the women of America have co-operated loyally. We are all in home army; the home army here must help the fighting forces and home armies over the 120 million Allies must eat.

American women were partners in feeding the world.
Freeborn County Standard, July 18th, 1918.

POLICE
TAKE NOTICE

Any Rioter Who Resents . Seeing

"THE KAISER"

The Beast of Berlin

Is an Enemy to America

We have instructed people who go to see this picture to instantly report any person who makes unfriendly remarks against the United States. KEEP YOUR EYES OPEN. We must crush the enemy within our gates. This picture will help seek them out. SEE IT. 'Twill make your blood boil.

METROPOLITAN

Thursday and Friday, July 4th and 5th

Three Big Shows Daily—3:00-7:30-9:00

Prices 10c and 25c, Includes War Tax

Lurid movie advertisement for "The Beast of Berlin."

Daily People's Press, July 3rd, 1918.

EPILOGUE

"Germany Surrenders
Peace Conference Now In Session"
—Freeborn County Standard,
November 7th, 1918

"German Envoys Accept Allied Terms Of Truce"
—The Daily People's Press,
November 12th, 1918

"Austin Went Wild"
—Austin Mayor George Hirsch,
November 12th, 1918

"Democracy Has Won Victory-Peace-Safety"
—Blooming Prairie Times,
November 14th, 1918

Freeborn County Standard.

VOL. 63, No. 87. ALBERT LEA, MINNESOTA, THURSDAY, NOV. 7, 1918 Established 1857

GERMANY SURRENDERS

PEACE CONFERENCE IS NOW IN SESSION

Enemy Accepts All of Allied Terms of Armistice---Soldiers Have Laid Down Arms---Fighting Ceased at 2 o'clock Our Time — Greatest War of History Brought to Abrupt End-- Marshall Foch Personally Dictates Terms to Hun Armistice Delegation.

Collapse of Military Power of Central Empires is Complete---Full Terms of Armistice Not Yet Known, But Are Said to Be More Harsh Than Austrian Terms---Military Decision Was Only Matter of Few Days When Capitulation Came.

B. N. Anderson Elected State Senator; Emmons Chosen Representative

Few Contests on County Ticket Provide

AUTO TIPOVER NEARLY COSTS LIVES

LARGE INTERESTS BUY LOCAL FACTORY

PLANT AND BUSINESS OF AMERICAN CULVERT COMPANY SOLD TO HUDSON MANUFACTURING CO.

People Everywhere Wildly Celebrating

The fall of autocracy, the fall of the Kaiser and the triumph of Democracy is being wildly celebrated in every part of the country today. In Albert Lea, in spite of a downpour of rain, hundreds of people appeared on Broadway at the call of the whistles. Autos, trucks, and even moving vans, formed an impromptu parade up

False Armistice.
Freeborn County Standard,
November 7th, 1918.

No Confirmation Yet." It must have been frustrating to learn that the report was false. Doughboys were still dying in France. Four days later, Germany signed an armistice agreement. On November 11th at 11 a.m. it went into effect, and people were able to celebrate for real. Communities, large and small, held victory celebrations. Church Bells pealed. Speeches, parades, and patriotic music were the order of the day. Austin mayor George Hirsch described the scene in a letter to his son a week after the armistice: "Austin went wild." He could have been describing almost any town in America.

Armistice celebrations could not completely erase the war's pain. The flu was still decimating the population and some families had yet to receive news of a loved one killed in action. Still, for survivors, life went on, as it always does.

There was a fifth and final liberty loan, and sometimes "slackers" were still hounded by their neighbors. It took time, but here at home, the old wounds did finally begin to heal.

The war ended with one final tragedy. Perhaps, it was the greatest tragedy of all. In spite of all the sacrifices, the millions dead and the terrible destruction, the war solved nothing. The vanquished nations still nursed the same grudges that caused the war in the first place. President Wilson's goal of a world made safe for democracy never came to pass. In the United States,

GEORGE HIRSH, Mayor FAY R. SMITH, City Recorder

Aldermen—O. W. OBERG, Alderman-At-Large, C. F. FOX, C. V. MOSSEY, E. B. CARTER, O. N. PECK, JACOB HERZOG, D. J. DENEEN

City of Austin

Austin, Minn., Nov. 12th 1918

Dear Alex.

Congratulations on your having been selected for
Officers training School. I suppose next will be Lieutenant Hirsh
We were all glad to hear from you. Could not write till we knew
your address. Post office closed at noon yesterday. Everybody celebrated.
Everybody was happy and had a good time. Stores and shops
closed at 3. P.M. School was dismissed for all day. I got a win
at 5.15 Monday morning and ordered all Whistles blown at
once. Austin went wild. The Mayor was as big a kid
as anybody. Came home this morning at 1.15 The Council and
Mayor and a few invited guests had a Midnight feast at
the Elk Hotel. It was great. Today seems very quiet. Just
returned from the Decker-Patterson auction sale, bought a few
Cows. Customers are coming and must quit Let us hear from
you often. All fine here. With love

Pa.

George Anderson wants you to look up Dr Carl Johnson
who married a sister to George's wife. I think you remember
him. J.C. Johnson's boy. You find his name in the Telephone
book.

"Austin Went Wild"
Austin Mayor George Hirsch to son Alex on November 12th, 1918.
Mower County Historical Society.

nationalistic isolationism was popular. Many Americans did not want to get entangled in another European war. The U.S. never joined the League of Nations, and without the support of the world's most powerful and wealthy nation, the League was weak. Eleven years after the armistice, the Great Depression swept across the world and authoritarians came to power in Germany and Japan. Soon the world would be at war again.

ACKNOWLEDGEMENTS

THIS BOOK WOULD HAVE BEEN impossible to write without the help of many people. First, my wife Harriet. Harriet assisted me in many ways. Most importantly, she always believed in, and supported, a frequently impatient, and grumpy, historian husband. Without her, the book would not have been written.

My friend Rick Herreid was instrumental in the project. Rick and I shared a common interest in World War One, and he suggested the project to me. He read and commented on several chapters, and he generously allowed me to use primary source information concerning his grandfather Myron, a decorated World War I marine. Rick even allowed me to fire his Springfield "03" World War I era rifle. Over the years we had many conversations about the war, often those talks helped bring blurred issues into focus. On two occasions, along with our wives Harriet and Karen, we visited World War One sites in France, Belgium, Central Europe, Bosnia and Serbia. No amount of reading and research can replace travel as a learning experience, and those visits played an important part in broadening my understanding of the conduct, and tragedy, of the war. Sadly, Rick died in 2019. I will always treasure his friendship and advice.

At Riverland Community College, my faculty friends and colleagues assisted in important ways. In the library, Keith Cich, helped me locate several obscure books and articles. Sharon Hyland read and commented on several chapters. Dr. Richard Campbell read and helped with much of the text. My Riverland friends, Scott, Heidi, Tom, Catherine, and Suzette pitched in with much needed moral support and encouragement. Karen Herreid allowed me to use her pictures of important sites in France.

I was pleasantly surprised at the amount of primary source material that was made available to me when word got out about the project. Judy Bungum, Esther Anthonisen, Paulette Hagan, and Doug and Pam Ruble all allowed me to use family letters and artifacts.

In Austin, Holly Johnson, director of the Hormel Historic Home provided access to Jay Hormel's war records, and, on several occasions, Holly gave me a forum to speak at History Happy Hour. My friend, Pat Stevens, opened the records of the Ladies Floral Club to me.

In Blooming Prairie, librarian and historian Nancy Vaillancourt helped with information about the saloons there during the war. She also gave me a forum to share my research. The forum opened new sources of information as residents shared information about their families. As a published author, Nancy's advice was much appreciated.

Local historical societies proved to be invaluable sources of information. I found the staff at all historical societies to be friendly, helpful, and enthusiastic about the project.

At the Freeborn County Historical Society, librarian Linda Evenson helped me locate information about wartime activities in Albert Lea and Freeborn County. Executive Director Stephanie Kibler supported the project and invited me to speak about it at a Freeborn County history forum.

At the Mower County Historical Society, archivist Sue Doocy was always ready to help, frequently pointing me in the right direction. Sue's vast knowledge of Mower County history proved to be a big help in my research. I do not know anyone who knows more local history than Sue. Jamie Timm and Randy Forster also provided support and encouragement along the way.

At the Steele County Historical Society, Archives and Technology Manager Daniel Moeckly provided me with electronic copies of letters written by Steele County soldiers to their families at home. Those letters proved to be a priceless source of firsthand information about the draft, training, and life on the Western Front. I was also invited to speak at the opening of the Steele County World War I exhibit.

To all who strive to keep memories of the past alive, thank you! Your mission is important.

BIBLIOGRAPHY

Newspapers and Periodicals:

Austin Daily Herald

Austin Weekly Herald

Blooming Prairie Times

Daily People's Press (Owatonna)

Ellendale Eagle

Freeborn County Standard

Minneapolis Tribune

Mower County Transcript

Mower County Transcript-Republican

The Nonpartisan Leader

Owatonna Journal-Chronicle

People's Press (Owatonna)

Princeton Union

The Farmer

Books, Diaries, Letters, Journals, Speeches, Government Documents, Maps, Illustrations:

American Battle Monuments Commission. ambc.gov.

Angell, Norman. *The Great Illusion: A Study of the Relation of Military Power to National Advantage*. New York: G.P. Putnam's sons, 1910.

Becket, Ian F.W. "The British Army and Conduct of Warfare, 1914-1918" Seminar, MIT, October 9th, 2002.

Beltrame, Achille, artist. "The assassination of Franz Ferdinand," *Domenica del Corriere*, July 12th, 1914. Illustration.

Berg, A. Scott. *Wilson*. New York: G.P. Putnam's Sons, 2013.

Berman, Hy. "Spies, armed militia and suspended civil rights in WW1 Minnesota," https://www.mprnews.org/story/2017/04/06/.

Berryman, Clifford Kennedy, artist. "I've Had About Enough of This," *Washington Evening Star*, March 10th, 1916. Illustration.

Blegen, Theodore Christian. *Minnesota: A History of the State*. Minneapolis: University of Minnesota Press, 1963.

Brandt, Allan M. *No Magic Bullet: A Social History of Venereal Disease in the United States Since 1880*. Oxford: Oxford University Press, 1987.

Brooks, Van Wyck. *The Confident Years: 1885-1915*. New York: Dutton, 1955.

Brown, Curt. *Minnesota 1918: When Flu, Fire, and War Ravaged the State*. St. Paul: Minnesota Historical Society Press, 2018.

Burnquist J.A.A. et al. *Report of Minnesota Commission of Public Safety*. St. Paul: Louis P. Dow Co.

Byerly, Carol R. "The U.S. Military and the Influenza Pandemic of 1918-1919," *Public Health Reports*, 125, Supplement 23 (2010): 82-91.

Chrislock, Carl Henry. *Ethnicity Challenged: The Upper Midwest Norwegian-American Experience in World War I*. Northfield, Minn.: Norwegian-American Historical Association, 1981.

Chrislock, Carl Henry. *The Progressive Era in Minnesota*. St. Paul: Minnesota Historical Society Press, 1971.

Chrislock, Carl Henry. *Watchdog of Loyalty: The Minnesota Commission of Public Safety During World War I,* St. Paul: Minnesota Historical Society Press, 1991.

Committee on Public Information: Four Minute Men Division. *Sample Speech.* Washington D.C., 1917.

Constitute Project. *United States of America 1789 (rev. 1992).* https://www.constituteproject.org.

Dayer, Roberta A. "Strange Bedfellows: JP Morgan & Co., Whitehall and the Wilson Administration during World War One," *Business History,* 18, no. 2 (1976).

Doenecke, Justus D. *Nothing Less Than War: A New History of America's Entry into World War I.* The University Press of Kentucky, 2011.

Dougherty, Richard. *In Quest of Quality: Hormel's First 75 Years.* Austin, George A. Hormel and Company, 1966.

Dunn, Elizabeth. *Letters to Walter Dunn.* Winterton England: 1914-1919. Dean Ulland, private collection.

Eighmey, Rae Katherine. *Food Will Win the War: Minnesota Crops, Cooks, and Conservation During World War I.* St. Paul: Minnesota Historical Society Press, 2010.

Ellis, John. *Eye-deep in Hell: Trench Warfare in World War I.* New York: Pantheon Books, 1976.

EUROPE, 1914 - Lines Drawn. United States Military Academy Department of History. Map.

Fleming, J. F. et. al., *The Cooperative Manager and Farmer*, 7, no.1 (September 1917) 1.

Gaston, Herbert E. *The Nonpartisan League*. New York: Harcourt, Brace and Howe, 1920.

Gregory, Ross. *The Origins of American Intervention in the First World War*. New York: Norton, 1971.

Gregory, Ross. *The Origins of American Intervention in the First World War*. New York: W.W. Norton and Company, 1971.

Grey, Edward (Grey of Fallodon). *Twenty-Five Years: 1892–1916*. New York: Frederick A. Stokes Company, 1925.

Grunklee, Herman. *Letters to family*. 1918. Steele County Historical Society.

Hall, Richard C. *Consumed by War: European Conflict in the 20th Century*. Lexington: The University Press of Kentucky, 2010.

Harding, Nelson, artist. "The Chain of Friendship," *Brooklyn Eagle*, December 4th, 1912. Illustration.

Hartmann, Walter. *Diary*. Austin: Mower County Historical Society, 1918.

Herreid, Karen, photographer. Multiple pictures of sites in France.

Herreid, Myron. *Diary*, November 9th, 1917. Rick Herreid, private collection.

Herwig, Holger H. *The First World War: Germany and Austria-Hungary 1914-1918*. London: Bloomsbury, 2014.

Hirsch, George. Letter to son Alex. November 12th, 1918. Mower County Historical Society.

Holbrook, Franklin Fisk, and Livia Appel. *Minnesota in the War with Germany*. St. Paul: Minnesota Historical Society, 1928.

Hough, Emerson. *The Web*. Chicago: The Reilly and Lee Company, 1919. https://www.archives.gov/files/education/lessons/sow-seeds/images/be-patriotic.gif

Jackson, Julian. *De Gaulle*. Cambridge, Massachusetts: Belknap Press of Harvard University Press, 2018.

Jay Hormel's draft registration card. Mower County, Minnesota. *Ancestry.com*. Accessed October 27th, 2020. http://www.ancestry.com.

Jenson, Carol E. *Agrarian Pioneer in Civil Liberties: The Nonpartisan League in Minnesota During World War I*. New York: Garland, 1986.

Jenson, Carol E. "Loyalty as a Political Weapon: The 1918 Campaign in Minnesota." *Minnesota History*, Spring, 1972.

John J. Pershing. "Belleau Wood" *Marines*, October 27th, 2020, https://www.6thmarines.marines.mil.

Keegan, John. *The First World War*. New York: Vintage Books, 2000.

Kennedy, David M. *Over Here: The First World War and American Society*. Oxford: Oxford University Press, 1980.

Kimble, James J. *Mobilizing the Home Front: War Bonds and Domestic Propaganda*. College Station: Texas A&M University Press, 2006.

Lafore, Laurence Davis. *The Long Fuse: An Interpretation of the Origins of World War I*. New York: J.P. Lippincott, 1965.

Lansing, Michael. *Insurgent Democracy; The Nonpartisan League in North American Politics.* Chicago: University of Chicago Press, 2015.

Larson, Bruce L. *Lindbergh of Minnesota: A Political Biography.* New York: Harcourt Brace Jovanovich, 1973.

Lass, William. *Minnesota: A History.* New York: W.W. Norton, 1998.

Lindbergh, Charles A. Sr. *Your Country at War and What Happens to You After a War.* Philadelphia: Dorrance & Company, 1934.

Lynch, Reah Jennette, compiler. *Win the War Cookboo*k. St. Louis: St. Louis County unit, Woman's committee, Council of national defense, Missouri division, 1917.

McGee, John F. *Letter to Minnesota Commission of Public Safety.* 1918.

Minnesota War Records Commission. *Edwin Jolson Military Service Record,* 1918.

Morlan, Robert L. *Political Prairie Fire: The Nonpartisan League, 1915-1922.*

Nicholsen, J.N. et.al. *Mower County in the World War.* John H. and Gertrude E. Skinner eds. Austin Minnesota: *Austin Herald,* 1919.

Nikolaki, Z. P., artist. *Hello! This is liberty speaking - billions of dollars are needed and needed now* / Z.P. Nikolaki. United States, 1918. Photograph. https://www.loc.gov/item/93502270/.

Northwest Europe, 1914, Western Front, The Schlieffen Plan and the French Plan. United States Military Academy Department of History. Map.

Palmer Narveson's draft registration card. Freeborn County,

Minnesota. *Ancestry.com.* Accessed October 27th, 2020. http://www.ancestry.com.

Partridge, O.V. *Letters to family*. 1918.

Pearl, Raymond, and Magdalen H. Burger. "Retail Prices of Food During 1917 and 1918." *Publications of the American Statistical Association,* 16, no. 127 (1919): 411-39. Accessed November 2nd, 2020. doi:10.2307/2964812.

Peat, Harold R. *Private Peat.* New York: Grosett and Dunlap, 1917.

Peterson, Wilbur. *I Went to War.* Marshall: The Messenger Press, 1938.

Richard Abeld's draft registration card. Mower County, Minnesota. *Ancestry.com.* Accessed October 27th, 2020. http://www.ancestry.com.

Picture of boy attending Mower County Fair, 1914. Daniel Cafourek.

Rhinow, W.F. *Report of the Adjutant General of the State of Minnesota,* vol.1 Minneapolis: Syndicate Printing, 1918.

Roosevelt, Theodore. *Letter to John Lorimo*r. Sharpnell.Org. Manuscript-Lusitania, 2015.

Roth, Joseph. *The Radetzky March.* London: Granta Books, 2003.

Severson, Harold. *Blooming Prairie Updat*e. Blooming Prairie: First National Bank of Blooming Prairie, 1980.

Seymour, Charles. *Woodrow Wilson and the World War: A Chronicle of Our Own Times.* New York: United States Publishers Association, 1921.

Stahr, Paul, artist. "Be Patriotic - sign your country's pledge to save the food," Library of Congress Prints and Photographs Division Washington, D.C., 1918. Illustration.

Stenger, SSgt Dieter. "The German Defensive Plan at Belleau Wood," *Doughboy Center*, accessed November 1st, 2020. http://www.worldwar1.com.

The Pillsbury Cookbook. Minneapolis: The Pillsbury Flour Mills Co., 1914.

Toland, John. *No Man's Land*. New York: Konecky and Konecky, 1980.

Tuchman, Barbara W. *The Zimmermann Telegram*. New York: Ballantine Books by arrangement with Macmillan Publishing Company, 1985.

Wilson, Woodrow. "Address to Congress Regarding Unrestricted U-Boat Warfare." Washington D.C. 1917.

Wilson, Woodrow. "Declaration of Neutrality." Washington D.C. 1914.

Wilson, Woodrow. "War message to Congress," Washington D.C., April 2nd, 1917.

Wood, C.E., compiler. *In the World War 1917-1918-1919: Freeborn County Minnesota*. Albert Lea: Albert Lea Publishing Company, 1919.

Zinn, Howard. *A People's History of the United States:1492-Present*. New York: Perennial Classics, 1999.

"After a Zeppelin Raid in London: "But Mother Had Done Nothing Wrong, Had She, Daddy?" Prevent this in New York: Invest in Liberty Bonds." Louis Raemaekers, propaganda, 1917. Rutgers University Library collection.

"Charles A. Lindbergh - Farmer-Labor Candidate for Governor of Minnesota," *The Nonpartisan Leader*, May 6th, 1918. Minnesota Historical Society.

"German U-boat UB-14 on the Black Sea 1918." DeGolyer Library, Southern Methodist University.

"Hoover Pledge," multiple publications, 1917.

"Red Blooded Men." 1917 Recruitment poster. Minnesota Historical Society.

"The Greatest Mother in the World," Red Cross advertisement, *Blooming Prairie Times*, May 16th, 1918.

"The Temptation," *Dallas Morning News*, March 2nd, 1917. Illustration.

"US Army Divisions in The Great War," *Global Security*, accessed October 27th, 2020. https://www.globalsecurity.org.

ABOUT THE AUTHOR

DEAN ULLAND is a retired History/Political Science professor with undergraduate degrees in History and Political Science. He holds an MA in History from Minnesota State, and taught for 18 years at Riverland Community College. Along with his wife, Dean lives on a farm near Corning, MN. They have 3 children and 8 grandchildren.

Throughout Dean's life, he has always had a passion for history and agriculture. His writing and research interests include local and Minnesota history, immigration history, World War I, and modern England. Dean's hobby is collecting rare books, and he has a large collection of old books and other documents, including many from southern Minnesota. Although no longer teaching, Dean continues to present his research at history conferences, and history programs in Austin, Rochester, Owatonna, Blooming Prairie, and Albert Lea, MN.

Dean's MA thesis, *The Reform of the House of Lords: The Parliament Act of 1911*, was nominated for the Midwest Association of Graduate Schools Distinguished Thesis Award.

Photo credit: Hannah Rosholt Photography - Austin, MN